Healing by HIS Spirit

GERALDINE D. BRYANT

ReadersMagnet, LLC

Healing by His Spirit
Copyright © 2020 by Geraldine D. Bryant

Published in the United States of America
ISBN Paperback: 978-1-950947-09-6
ISBN Hardback: 978-1-950947-13-3
ISBN eBook: 978-1-950947-08-9

All rights reserved. No part of this publication may be reproduced, stored in a retrieval system or transmitted in any way by any means, electronic, mechanical, photocopy, recording or otherwise without the prior permission of the author except as provided by USA copyright law.

Unless otherwise indicated, Bible quotations are taken from The King James Bible—Psalm 35 and the New Living Translation of the Holy Bible, Copyright © 1996.

The opinions expressed by the author are not necessarily those of ReadersMagnet, LLC.

ReadersMagnet, LLC
10620 Treena Street, Suite 230 | San Diego, California, 92131 USA
1.619.354.2643 | www.readersmagnet.com

Book design copyright © 2020 by ReadersMagnet, LLC. All rights reserved.
Cover design by Ericka Walker
Interior design by Shemaryl Evans

ACKNOWLEDGEMENT

Special thanks to JoAnne Gee for her contribution in the preparation of this work.

DEDICATED

In loving memory of my mother

MARY FRANCES TATE
(1913–2005)

Whom I owe my deepest gratitude for believing in me;
That I can do anything I set my mind to do.

FOREWORD

I MUST ADMIT AT THE OUTSET that this autobiography by Ms. Geraldine Bryant is one of the best I've read in recent years.

I strongly recommend this book to older youths to sharpen their sensitivity to certain evils at their respective age levels regardless of class, race or ethnic origin. I further recommend it to men and women to sharpen their awareness of how their attitudes and behaviors can throw innocent and well–meaning persons off course and to destruction.

You will note in reading this book how Ms. Bryant responded creatively to the challenges of life's negativities that she encountered.

She experienced what the Danish philosopher, Soren Kierkegaard called three "stages on life's way" (aesthetical or pleasure, the ethical or conventional morality and religion B—Christianity in particular). Though the religious stage eventually became predominant in her life, yet these stages were somewhat simultaneous.

It is also interesting to note how towards the end of the book the religious stage is the result of her own "purpose driven life" and concludes with making her body a "living sacrifice to God," a "monastery of the heart," in her horizontal reach to others and her vertical relation to God as revealed through Jesus Christ.

Finally, I recommend this book to Christians and non-Christians alike. Ms. Bryant has demonstrated in her own life the stubborn decision to opt for "the courage to be" amid negative influences in her life. She now encourages others to accept "God's acceptance" for those who feel unacceptable. Her story is one of emergence from wounded victim to wounded healer.

George Thompson, Jr. Ph.D., D.D.
Pastor Emeritus and
Professor Emeritus

CHAPTER 1

I LIVED IN A THREE STORY semidetached house shared with my mother, father, grandfather and an elderly woman, of no relation, who occupied the third floor, situated on a beautiful tree lined street in the West Mt. Airy section of Philadelphia. The neighborhood seemed quite quiet, unlike the former area I moved from. Beautiful red and pink rose bushes draped over the hedges, making it the most attractive front yard on the block.

We moved here because my grandfather lost his eyesight and needed help. My mother was only too willing to come and look after him. She was his only daughter and his second wife had passed away a few years earlier. Moving to a new neighborhood was scary. I didn't know anyone and I felt isolated. I missed being around my friends whom I grew up with, therefore, I spent many lonely days in my room. Helping my mother with chores around the house filled in many hours of otherwise, pure boredom. My room was my safe haven, shut away from the rest of the world.

I glanced around my cluttered room. My eyes focused on the walls. They were painted olive green. How ugly, I thought. Most girls my age liked pastels and bright, pretty colors. I couldn't believe I had chosen such a horrible green. What in the world was I thinking of? I shook my head in disgust. Despite the gloomy, dull color surrounding me, I loved the solitude my bedroom afforded me. This was where I found myself when I wanted to daydream or to just connect with my inner being.

I was fourteen years old, a ninth grader and three years from senior high graduation. My interests bordered on writing and journalism. Like many girls, I dreamed of having a great career, falling in love, getting married and having children, but in that order.

The prospect of attending college eluded me. My parents couldn't afford it. Anything short of a fully paid scholarship was out of the question. I sensed early on that money, or the lack thereof, was an issue within my family. Often I would hear my mom and dad arguing over money matters. My mother sacrificed much to get me things comparable to what other children had. More importantly though, I was a very grateful child and anything my parents did for me, I deeply appreciated.

I had two brothers. They were much older than I, twenty-six and twenty-four years respectively. Jimmy and Skeeter, as he was affectionately known, were both in the military around the time I was born. I was a change of life baby entering the world when my mother was forty-one years old. My brothers didn't live at home, therefore, I felt like an only child.

Whenever the family gathered for holiday celebrations my brothers would share with me what their lives were like when they were young. My oldest brother, in particular, would speak of the times during the depression era when food was scarce. He would relate how they were always fed first and how mom and grandmother would eat the leftover scraps from their plates. I never had the opportunity to meet this loving grandmother they spoke so fondly of. She passed away ten years before my birth. How I wished I could have known her.

I sat on my vanity stool, staring at my reflection in the mirror, my hair in disarray, as I contemplated my agenda for today. I sat lost in thought for several minutes, which was quickly interrupted by the sound of a lawn mower whirring in the distance.

My attention shifted to my clothes strewn around the room. I rose from the stool and picked them up piece by piece, neatly folding them in a pile on a nearby chair. As the noise from the mower grew louder, I realized it was coming from my own backyard. I remembered my mother telling me a few days earlier that she had hired a neighborhood boy to cut the grass. I walked over to the window and drew the curtain aside to get a better view of the boy I longed to see up close. This was my opportunity to really focus in on his physical features. From the window, the only thing visible was the top of his head.

I descended the stairs and walked toward the back of the house. The kitchen inside door was ajar allowing me to approach the screen door undetected. I slowly eased the door open and watched for several minutes as he pushed the mower forward, oblivious of my presence.

Finally Sidney glanced up and noticed me staring at him. "Hello," he muttered, nodding his head.

I waved my hand with a smile. "Hi Sidney," I responded.

Sidney had a nice medium brown skin tone and a well groomed afro. He was of medium weight with good muscular arms. He was considered to be the most popular boy in the neighborhood and probably already had a girlfriend.

When Sidney had finished his work, he shut the mower off, sat down on the steps to rest and invited me to join him. I offered him a glass of water which he gladly accepted. We talked for several minutes. Finally Sidney rose to his feet and indicated he had to leave but before he left we exchanged phone numbers.

"Thanks for the drink," he said handing me the empty glass.

"You're welcome," I replied." He waved goodbye and promised to call me.

I watched Sidney as he grasped the handle of the mower and rolled it carefully out of the gate. I slowly closed the back door, excited that I had finally got the chance to see Sidney up close and to talk with him. I don't really know why I had such an overwhelming attraction for him but I had this strong urge to find out more about him. I returned to my room, anticipating on hearing from him soon.

Two days later my phone rang. I picked up the receiver. Sidney was on the other end of the line. I was excited to hear his voice. After conversing a few minutes we agreed to meet on my front steps. I hurried down the stairs and anxiously awaited his arrival. Several minutes later I saw Sidney emerge from his doorway. I glanced up as he approached. I was very inquisitive and I asked Sidney many questions about himself. He proceeded to tell me that his uncle had taken him under his wing and was teaching him the mortician business.

"Ugh!" I replied. "You handle dead people. Do you really like that kind of work?" I asked.

"Yeah," Sidney replied.

He began to tell me all the ins and outs of the business. He was so excited about it. I listened intently. I just couldn't wrap my mind around that particular profession, but it was great to hear the enthusiasm in his voice when he talked about it.

After that day Sidney and I started seeing each other. Our dates consisted of sitting on the porch and walking around the neighborhood. We never went to a party nor a movie.

A few weeks later I was walking home. I had just stepped off the trolley car. As I neared the corner of my street I noticed a group of girls gathered around the steps of a corner house. I had seen them many times before. They weren't friendly and they didn't welcome me to the neighborhood. I felt as if I were invading their turf. They constantly poked fun at me and made snide remarks as I passed by.

"Here comes Miss Holy," they remarked.

I pretended not to hear them as I clutched my Bible in my hand, totally ignoring them. I passed them like they weren't even there, careful not to make eye contact with them. I had a purpose and goal for my life and it certainly wasn't about hanging out on street corners doing nothing.

Later that evening I met up with Sidney. I questioned him about the group of girls in the neighborhood. I told him that they didn't like me and made nasty remarks.

"Don't worry about those girls, they're just jealous," he said.

"They're jealous of what…me? They don't even know me," I replied.

"Just don't pay any attention to them," he added. Sidney seemed unconcerned to say the least.

A few minutes later we changed the subject and moved on to something else. An hour later I was headed up the steps to my porch. After bidding farewell to Sidney I swung the door open and entered the foyer. Sidney was looking back at me as I slowly closed the door.

I attached myself to people who led church centered lives. I was active in my church since age six, attending Sunday school on a regular basis. At age eleven I accepted Jesus Christ as my personal Lord and Savior and was baptized on May 1, 1966. My church life is what sustained me during the puberty years. It kept me out of trouble. Church had so much to offer. I enjoyed the many religious activities such as singing on the choir, attending the BTU (Baptist Training Union) classes, performing in drama skits, attending Vacation Bible School, caroling in the streets at Christmastime and going to parties hosted by our choir director and sometimes other adults in charge of the youth groups.

The following week I received a call from one of my friends that a teenage boy was killed in a gang related incident. The young adult choir was asked to sing for the funeral service. My heart skipped a beat. I had never been to anyone's funeral before and I wasn't sure I wanted to go to this one. My heart was heavy because the decedent was a friend of one of the choir members. At that point I realized that I had to make an honest effort to be there for her support.

The next time I saw Sidney I was telling him that I had to sing for the funeral.

"I know who you're talking about. My uncle has the body."

He noticed the uneasiness I felt as we talked about it. He assured me everything would be all right.

"You will be coming home with me after the service."

I looked at him perplexed. "You will be in the funeral car with your uncle," I said.

"That's okay. You can get in the car with us and we will take you home. Don't worry so much about everything."

I smiled at Sidney's reassurance. He was very attentive when he wanted to be.

The night of the funeral was upon me. I hurriedly got dressed in my black and white attire. When I arrived at the church there were several people lined up to view the body. I stood inside the vestibule to prepare for the procession of the choir. No one wanted to lead the line in. Finally someone pushed me to the front of the line. I stood there trying to gather my wits. I was shaking like a leaf. I focused my eyes to the front center of the sanctuary where the casket rested. Sidney stood at the foot of the coffin while his uncle stood on the opposite end. Once he noticed me, he came up the aisle towards me, leaned forward and whispered in my ear.

"Relax. Everything is going to be all right." He touched my arm lightly and returned to his post.

A few minutes later the choir walked down the aisle in single file and entered the choir loft. Once seated in place, the service began. The minister led the family members down the aisle, reciting the 23rd Psalm. As I sat throughout the service, the tension began to ease. When the service was over I waited for Sidney in the vestibule. The church was nearly empty when he approached me. He wrapped his arm around my shoulder and led me out of the church to the waiting limo. I got in the front seat and Sidney slid in next to me. He formally introduced me to his uncle, even though I already knew of him. He glanced over at me.

"Are you okay?" Sidney asked.

"Yes, I'm fine," I replied.

The limo slowly pulled away from the curb and headed towards Germantown Avenue. The traffic light was red as we approached the corner. When the light changed to green, Sidney's uncle made a right turn. With fingers entwined in each other's hands I felt so comforted by Sidney's warmth and attentiveness. He looked into my eyes and leaned over to kiss me on my lips. It was the best kiss he ever gave me. I melted in his arms. It was at that moment that I realized I was very much in love with him. I rested my head on Sidney's shoulder as he pulled me closer to him. At the same time, I was hoping his uncle had not noticed the secret kiss we stole as he headed up the avenue. Sidney and I continued to see each other over the next several weeks. I was very happy that he enjoyed spending time with me.

One day he called me to ask if he could come over to see me.

"Sidney, you know I'm not allowed to have company when my mother isn't home."

"It's just for a few minutes. I won't stay long."

"No Sidney, my grandfather is here and you know how he is. He can't see but he sure can hear." After a little more persuasion on his part, I agreed.

"Come to the back door," I instructed him.

"Okay," Sidney agreed.

I waited at the back door for Sidney to arrive. When he approached, I held my finger to my lips indicating hush mode.

"What's up Sidney?" I asked in a low pitch voice.

"I just wanted to see you and hold you in my arms for a few minutes," he replied.

Quietly Sidney slipped through the door and reached for me. He kissed me gently and pulled me close to him. For several minutes we embraced each other. As things began to get more intense, I backed up.

"I am fourteen years old and you are sixteen. You are too young as well," I said.

He insisted he knew what he was doing.

I said to him, "No Sidney," as I removed his hands from around my waist. "I am not ready to take this relationship to the next level."

I was full of emotion but I didn't back down. His eyes narrowed as he stared at me. I could see the disappointment in his face as I pulled away from him.

His parting words were, "call me when you're older."

As I watched him turn to leave, my heart started breaking. I had deep feelings for Sidney but was it real love or just crazy infatuation? Every part of my being screamed yes it's real. A tear rolled down my cheek. The next instant, Sidney was gone. One thing was for certain; I didn't regret the choice I made that day.

I stood in the doorway for several minutes, lost in thought when I heard my grandfather approaching.

"Who's in here? I heard voices," he said.

"There's no one here, grandfather," I replied.

He turned and headed back to his room, mumbling as he went. As the tears welled in my eyes, I slowly closed the door and a chapter in my life.

September was fast approaching. It was time to think about going back to school. It was very hard for me to concentrate on school. The relationship breakup with Sidney was constantly on my mind. I found it very difficult to move on and forget. My heart ached for his companionship but he was interested in other girls. I watched him parade them up and down the street on many occasions. I had to get use to the fact that we were no longer together. I suffered in silent humiliation alone, often shedding many tears but I knew I had to persevere.

Getting ahead and being at the top of my class was most important. I studied very hard, yet I couldn't maintain an A average. When I entered tenth grade I changed my studies to a commercial–academic curriculum. By now I was pretty sure I wasn't headed for college. I continued to do well and my B grades outnumbered the A's.

When I wasn't studying, I found myself visiting Dee-Dee. She was my best friend and we did a lot of things together. We would go to the avenue and shop. Once in a while on Fridays we would buy silver trout sandwiches. They were so delicious. Sometimes I would accompany her when she went out to sell handbags and purses which her father made for a living. Whatever we found ourselves involved in, we enjoyed it.

One day on my way home from Dee-Dee's house I encountered the same group of girls who constantly annoyed me. I was halfway down the block before I realized it was them. It was too late to turn around and go in the opposite direction so I pressed on. As I got closer to them, one girl stepped out in front of me. I was pretty sure she was the leader of the gang. I stopped short. The other girls moved closer to me as well.

"We want to meet with you on the corner at five o'clock tomorrow."

I looked at them and I responded. "Okay, see you tomorrow."

She stepped aside to let me pass and I continued around the corner to my house. I thought about what had just transpired. I agreed to a meeting with the girls. I had no backup. I was alone, yet I showed them no fear. What could possibly happen to me, other than, all of them jumping me to beat me up?

The next evening I walked to the corner we agreed to meet on at five o'clock in the evening. I left my house without telling my mother where I was going or what was happening. I slowly walked to the corner. No one was in sight. I leaned against the wall of a storefront building waiting for them to show. The minutes went by. I glanced at my watch. It was 5:15 p.m. I looked around in all directions. No one approached the corner. After a few more minutes I decided to return home. I was there and they were a no–show. Maybe they were watching me from a nearby window, I don't know. I never ran into those girls again. Each time I walked down the street they weren't out. Surely I thought God had kept me out of their path.

A new family moved into the neighborhood. I became friends with the Phillips. I felt more at ease. I had someone to communicate with. I had a new hang out. Their children were around my age and we went to the same high school.

Another young lady named Margie attended my church. I discovered that she also lived in my neighborhood. We became good friends as well.

I believed God had placed new people in my life. I was happy to finally feel like I was part of the neighborhood. I built lasting friendships with these people and that was a good thing.

One day my phone rang. Sidney was on the line. I was surprised and excited to hear from him. Two years had passed since the breakup. Since he lived across the street from me it was hard to avoid him entirely. I always spoke to him in passing but there wasn't much conversation otherwise. He called to rekindle the relationship. In that time frame my feelings for him had not diminished completely. We talked for hours. It was my hope that Sidney had matured somewhat in the two year absence. I wanted to take things slow and I didn't want to be pressured by his demands. With that understanding between the two of us, we started to date again. I noticed that he was still talking to other girls. I knew I had to deal with that at some point because they weren't completely out of the picture. I respected the fact that he was honest about it and not purposely trying to keep it from me.

During the months that followed, our relationship became rocky. I was getting tired of the ups and downs of our courtship, but my love for him kept me bouncing back and forth. As difficult as it was, I wasn't ready to give up on the relationship.

Almost a year later, Sidney decided to enlist in the Marines. I was sad to hear that he had done that. I was worried for his safety in the event he would be stationed overseas. He was his mother's only son. That didn't seem to bother him. He really wanted to go. He felt the service would mature him much more.

It wasn't long before Sidney was off to his six week basic training. I had a lot of time on my hands to seriously think about our relationship. It bothered me that we continued to break up and reunite over and over again. I needed some stability if this relationship was going to continue. I planned to sit down with Sidney once he returned home and we were going to have a heart-to-heart talk about everything. I didn't want him in and out of my life like a revolving door. Something had to change for sure.

When Sidney returned home six weeks later, we sat on the porch for a long time talking about our relationship and where it was headed. Neither one of us was ready for marriage so we steered away from conversations like that.

Sidney placed his arm around my shoulder.

"Everything is fine," he assured me. "I am being deployed to Vietnam. I have to serve two years. I will be leaving in a couple of weeks and will write you whenever I can," he added.

"Okay, but I am not happy about it," I replied.

It was early July 1971. I was seventeen years old. The time had come for Sidney to prepare for his overseas deployment. In a few days he would be gone. We spent a lot of time together before he left. I was so wrapped up in Sidney, I allowed my emotions to take control of me one day and I threw all of my principles out the window. I loved Sidney and I didn't hide it. I let him know how important he was to me. Sidney placed his hand in mine and led me to a place on his aunt's property where we could be alone. We talked a long while then he gently laid me on my back. He laid down beside me and we cuddled for a while. Then the lights went out.

I was happy and sad at the time, happy because I finally lost my virginity to the young man I was so in love with, but sad because I could never get it back. I finally understood what my mother meant when she said stay away from boys. Once it's gone, you can't reclaim it. I loved Sidney and I often told him so but he never uttered those beautiful words back to me. It suddenly hit me that maybe he didn't feel the same way about me. I was deeply hurt on the inside, yet we continued our courtship.

A few days later, Sidney was gone. He promised to write soon. I kissed him goodbye the night before. I didn't see him leave the next day. It was better that way.

The next few weeks were hard. I anxiously waited for the mailman to come. Day after day I rushed to the front door when I heard the mail drop through the slot. I gathered the mail in my hands, quickly flipping through it, looking for something from Sidney. There was nothing. A month had passed, still nothing. Frustration soon set in. Why wasn't he writing me after promising to do so?

One day I was sitting on my porch when I noticed Sidney's mother standing in her doorway. I hurried over to ask her if she had received any letters from Sidney since he left. She said no. His letters weren't getting through for some reason. I breathed a sigh of relief. With my mind at ease, I returned home believing that I would eventually hear from him.

CHAPTER 2

It was a typical hot day in early August. I walked to the avenue and waited for the trolley car. In the distance I could see it approaching. A few minutes later the car stopped in front of me. The doors opened. I stepped up to the coin box and dropped my fare in. Quickly glancing around, I slid into a seat by an open window. As the trolley began to move, my hair blew lightly in the soft summer breeze. I settled in for the fifteen minute ride.

I arrived at Dee-Dee's house. We spent hours sitting around the house and on the front porch reminiscing about our many escapades; just good old fashioned girl talk.

Shortly after 5:00 p.m. Dee-Dee's father appeared in the doorway. He stood there for several minutes. Finally he broke his silence.

Addressing me he uttered, "I want you to take a cab home when you are ready to leave."

I looked at him, puzzled, "Why a cab?" I asked.

"I don't want you traveling alone at night. I feel responsible for you while you're here."

"But, I take public transportation all the time and I'm always home before dark."

"I know," he said, "but I would feel much better if I knew you arrived home safely."

"Well, if you insist."

Something about today was different from any other day. I couldn't quite put my finger on it. Breaking my regular routine felt so out of place to me. I tried to dismiss the uneasiness I felt.

At 7:30 p.m. the cab rolled up, partially on the sidewalk, so as not to block the traffic, and waited for me to come out of the house.

I grabbed my purse and turned to say good-bye to Dee-Dee.

"I'll see you later, Dee-Dee."

"Okay, be careful and call me when you get home," she replied.

As I descended the steps, the cab driver got out and walked around the back of the cab. He opened the door for me. I climbed in the back seat, placing my purse next to me. He closed the door and hurried around to the driver side and slid beneath the wheel.

The cab driver started the engine. As the cab pulled off, I looked back to see Dee-Dee standing in the door, waving.

"Where to?" he asked.

I gave him the address and leaned back against the seat. The cabby introduced himself as Glen. He struck up a conversation almost immediately but I wasn't interested in idle chit-chat. I wasn't impressed at all. As he continued to converse on ridiculous subject matter, my mind drifted to Sidney, anxiously awaiting his return home from duty.

A few minutes later I noticed the cabby glancing at me through the rear view mirror several times as he drove. When he arrived at my house he asked me for my phone number.

"You don't need to know my number," I retorted.

I paid my fare and exited the cab. I ran up the steps and hurriedly turned the key in the lock. Once safely inside, I peered out the window. The cab was still there. He remained there for several minutes before taking off.

A few days later I was back at Dee-Dee's house hanging out like usual. It was early afternoon when Dee-Dee's younger sister ran into the house yelling.

"Did anybody call a cab?"

"No," Dee-Dee replied.

We both got up and went to the door.

"That's the cabby that picked me up a few nights ago. I wonder what he's doing here."

As I stepped onto the porch, Glen got out and came around to the bottom step.

"I thought I would check to see if you were here today since I was in the area. I would like to give you a ride home. It's free, no charge," he said smiling.

"No," I responded. "I'm not ready to leave."

"I can come back later when you are ready," he said.

I looked at him skeptically.

"I don't think so. I'll get home alright."

He pleadingly persisted until I gave in.

Being naïve as I was, his smooth mannerism deceived me. Seemingly harmless in his invitation, I agreed to go home in his cab.

A couple hours later Glen returned but he wasn't driving the cab. A bright lemon colored Dodge Demon sports car was parked on the sidewalk.

"Where's the cab?" I asked him.

"I had to turn it in. I am finished work for the day," he replied. "How do you like my car?"

"It's alright, I guess."

"Are you ready?"

"Yes, I think so," I nodded.

I climbed into the front seat of the car and rested my head against the cushioned seat as the car sped away from my girlfriend's house. That day, little did I know that my dreams for the future would be forever altered.

Two blocks from Dee-Dee's house, the car made a right turn. Glen pulled into a parking spot in front of a house and got out.

"I'll be right back. My family lives here and I need to check on something," he said.

I patiently waited about ten minutes before I thought of walking back to Dee-Dee's house. A few minutes later, Glen emerged.

"Come," he said. "I told my mother about you and she wants to meet you."

"Why? We are not dating or anything like that," I replied.

"I know, but I told her I met a nice young lady and she wants to meet you."

"Glen, I really don't see the point."

"Okay, then just say hi. It will only be a few minutes."

Reluctantly I allowed Glen to lead me by the hand and we ascended the stairs to the third floor. When we arrived at the top he pulled out a set of keys and unlocked the door. He entered and I followed. Once inside, I looked around the room. The first thing I noticed was a plate of half eaten food. It was covered in cobwebs. The rest of the room didn't look lived in neither. All of a sudden, a bell went off in my head and a strange feeling crept over me.

"I'll wait for you outside," I said.

I started to head for the door I came through and just as I was about to exit, Glen came up behind me and slammed the door shut.

"Where are you going?" he asked.

"I'm leaving," I replied. "No one lives here. This place is vacant."

"You are not leaving until I say so."

Glen became very forceful and controlling. The pleasantness he exuberated before was now gone. He had turned on me in an instant and became very demanding. I started to cry.

Glen snatched me by the arm and forced me down on a nearby bed. He quickly climbed on top of me as I struggled to break free. Glen grabbed my hands, locking them behind my back. I screamed in horror as he forced my legs apart and raped me for several minutes. He released one of his hands and covered my mouth to muffle my screams. When it was over, I was in a state of shock. I couldn't believe I fell for his ploy. I sat there on the bed, dazed. The tears fell freely, hard and fast. How could I be tricked like this? More to the point, how could I be so trusting and not see this coming? I was so distraught and I felt so stupid. I couldn't believe that I had seriously put myself in such a dangerous situation. Glen kept me by his side as he led me out the door. That day he held me captive for six hours, probably to prevent me from going to the police. He constantly threatened me over and over if I ever told anyone what transpired here.

Upon reflection, I now think that having older parents and brothers and lack of sex education programs in school or church, my ignorance was exploited. The cab driver coming to the residence without being called and the words "free and no charge" plus with his strong persistence should have cautioned me.

When Glen released me in front of my house, I ran up the steps heading straight for the bathroom, avoiding my mother in the process. I filled the tub with water and climbed in. I felt dirty and the more I tried to physically wash away the filth, the dirtier I felt.

After the bath I entered my room and laid across my bed in the dark for several minutes.

"Where were you God when I needed you today?"

Psalm 10:1 says – "O Lord, why do you stand so far away? Why do you hide when I need you the most?"

I felt so abandoned and alone. I couldn't feel His presence. He didn't protect me from this beast of a man. I closed my eyes for several seconds as tears trickled down my cheeks. The more I thought about it, the more I realized that God was there. When I thought of the alternative, Glen could have killed me and left me dead in an abandoned apartment, yet, I got out alive. I was truly blessed.

A few weeks passed since that traumatic day with Glen. I hadn't seen or heard from him but I sensed he was watching me from somewhere nearby. An uneasy feeling stayed with me day after day. I walked and lived in fear from that point on. I was constantly looking over my shoulder wherever I went. His threats resonated in my ears. I didn't tell my mother, my best friend or anyone else for that matter, about the rape. I felt doomed and cursed. I retreated into a shell and hid for several days. When I emerged, I was a changed person. I started living a lie.

One morning I awoke feeling very lightheaded. As I headed to the bathroom my stomach started churning. Nausea set in and I started gaging but my stomach was empty. I had very little to eat the day before. My menstrual cycle was late and a dreadful thought engulfed me. Could I be pregnant? I asked myself. I made an appointment at the clinic to take a pregnancy test. The results proved positive. I was devastated. Not only was I raped, but impregnated as well. I panicked. My life had turned upside down and I didn't know how to handle it.

I picked up the telephone and called the cab company where Glen worked. I asked several questions but they wouldn't release any information on him other than to confirm his name and that he worked there. Disappointed, I hung up.

A few days later, the telephone rang. I picked it up. Glen was on the other end of the line.

"Why did you call my job?" he asked.

"I am pregnant and you are responsible. I hate you for what you did to me," I cried.

I slammed the phone down and retreated to my room. There I sat contemplating what my next move would be. Many thoughts ran through my head. Should I have this baby? Should I have an abortion? Putting the baby up for adoption was not an option. I couldn't live with the knowledge of someone else raising my child. I would wonder if the baby was being treated well or if he or she was happy, not an option. Abortions were illegal in Pennsylvania and I would have to go to New York. That was not an option either. I decided I would keep my baby, raise the child myself and love him or her unconditionally. That was the correct option for me.

Hours later Glen showed up. I didn't want to talk to him. I said what I had to say over the phone. I decided that I didn't want him to have anything to do with my baby. I would be the responsible one. He was a stranger. I knew nothing about him, other than his name. He didn't deserve a place in my baby's life. He showed up whenever he felt like it, aggravating me constantly. He lurked around the neighborhood, spying on me and trying to watch my every move every chance he got.

My frequent visits to Dee-Dee's house became less and less. I didn't feel comfortable being around my friends anymore. I didn't want to have to explain things to them, things I wasn't ready to talk about. One day she asked me about Glen. I lied to my best friend and told her that I was dating Glen in order to justify the pregnancy. I wanted to tell her the truth about what happened. I just couldn't open up to her or anyone else for that matter, and so the lies started. I repeated the same thing to the Phillips and my good friend, Margie. No one knew the horrible secret I harbored.

I continued to go to school despite my condition. I couldn't fall behind in my school work and I wanted to graduate in June. This was a temporary setback. Some of the other pregnant girls at school were dropping out; not me. It made me push all the more to get ahead and stay ahead, even though I knew it would be challenging at times.

One afternoon the phone rang. I picked up the receiver. Glen was on the other end. He wanted to know what I was doing.

"I'm not doing anything. What do you want?" I asked.

"If I wasn't so far away I would come and check on you," he replied.

"I don't need you checking on me. Goodbye Glen." I hung up the phone.

Five minutes later I was sitting on my bed when I heard someone running up the stairs. I got up to look to see who had entered my house without knocking; then I realized that my front door was wide open. I often left the door open on nice days. The house wasn't air-conditioned.

Glen appeared at the top of the stairs. When I saw him I realized that the telephone conversation was a lie. Why did he pretend he was at the other end of town when he really called from somewhere close by?

"Where is he?" Glen demanded.

"Where is who? I asked.

"I know he is hiding somewhere."

"Glen, who are you looking for in my house?"

I sat down on my bed while Glen ran through the house, looking behind doors, in closets and under beds searching for whoever he thought was there.

After a fruitless search Glen returned to my room. He stooped down in front of me and demanded to know where the person was hiding in my house.

"You're crazy. As you can see, there is no one here."

I never saw it coming. In the next instant, Glen slapped me so hard across my face, breaking my glasses. As the lens shattered, a jagged edge cut me across the bridge of my nose. I screamed in pain. My head ached and blood trickled down my nose. In horror I sat there in disbelief. It was the only pair of glasses I had. He apologized afterwards. It was too late, the damage was done.

"Get out of my house and never come back," I shrieked. "Just get out!"

Glen left as quickly as he had come.

I ran to the door and locked it. As I climbed the stairs I turned my head to look in the direction of my father's room. He sat in a chair by the window, talking to himself, unaware of what just transpired. I noticed he had been drinking.

My father was an alcoholic, often in a drunken stupor, and seemingly unfazed by his surroundings.

When my mother came home I told her I needed new glasses. I didn't tell her that Glen slapped me and broke them. I was too afraid to let her know how he was treating me. He had a habit of instilling fear in me. He was very manipulative and he exercised total control whenever he could.

In my third month of pregnancy my mother noticed the changes occurring in my body. She never questioned me about it. She really didn't have to. Mothers know these things. I believed it was because she really didn't know how to talk about sensitive issues with me. I wouldn't begin to know how to approach her with it either.

Two weeks passed. It was Thanksgiving Day. My family gathered at my house for dinner. I sat on the floor watching TV. I heard my mother whispering to my brothers and sisters-in-law.

"She's pregnant," she whispered.

Everyone pretended not to notice my protruding bump. I was glad because I didn't want to talk about it. I wasn't able to reveal to them what happened so it was better that way. After dinner I returned to watching TV. My sisters-in-law, Christine and Mary, helped mom with clearing the table and my brothers sat around talking. I switched my program to the football game. I knew my brothers were anxious to watch the game, so I left the room and went upstairs.

It was early December. Glen came around the house flashing a large sum of money. He formed piles of fives, tens and twenties. Then he picked up each stack and counted them.

He turned to my mother and said, "I am going to pay the hospital bill for you when the time comes."

"That's nice of you, but I will make sure everything is taken care of," she responded.

Glen picked up the stacks of money, recounting it before placing it back in his wallet.

He hurried out the door. I looked at my mother.

"Don't believe for one minute that he is going to give you any money. He's showing off. You will never see that money again."

I ascended the stairs and returned to my room.

In mid-January Glen entered my house. The door was closed but unlocked. Under the circumstances I should have checked the door whenever I was alone in the house. As he pushed the door open he rang the bell to let me know he was entering.

I started down the stairs and found Glen staring up at me. His eyes darted back and forth and a devilish smirk plastered his face.

"Why are you here? You are not welcome in this house."

Glen was wearing a gold chain around his neck. Dangling from the chain was a devil holding a pitchfork. His car was parked directly in front of my house. I could see some lettering on the passenger side door that wasn't there before. The word "Demon" was displayed in big, bold, black letters. It was unnerving. The words, "devil," "pitchfork" and "demon" swirled in my head. I saw all of these as symbols of Satanism.

"Let yourself out, Glen. Please leave!" I ordered.

Instead, Glen chose to follow me upstairs.

I didn't trust Glen and I felt he was up to something whenever he was around. I just wanted him gone. When

Glen reached the top step he turned towards the bathroom. All of a sudden he snatched me by the arm and pulled me into the bathroom with him.

"Leave me alone, Glen. I don't want to be in here with you."

He picked me up like a garment you would hang on a hook and held me high against the door. I squirmed and twisted in his grip, but to no avail. Once again, he sexually molested me. When he was done he lowered me to the floor.

"See? I can do whatever I want to you, when I want. No one will ever love you," he snarled.

With a smug look of satisfaction that he once again had conquered, he left the house.

Hate is a strong word, which was never a part of my vocabulary; something I never felt for anyone, until now.

Glen continued to make a living hell of my life. He found new ways to aggravate me, taunt me, manipulate and play on my fears. The games he played were unending. I hated him with an unimaginable vengeance.

A few days later, the phone rang. I hesitated to answer, but not knowing, piqued my curiosity.

"Hello," I answered.

Immediately the voice of an angry young woman bellowed in my ears.

"Who is this?" I questioned.

"This is Glen's wife. I found your telephone number in his pocket and he told me all about you. He said you were easy, you just happened to be there, and he doesn't care anything about you," she shouted.

She continued to rant and rave for several minutes. I stood there speechless as she expressed herself until I got tired of listening to her. I heard a click in the line and realized my mother had picked up the downstairs extension. She started hollering at the young woman on the other end.

"Mom, please hang up the phone," I pleaded. "I can handle this."

A few seconds later I heard my mother slam the phone down after telling the woman to never call here again.

"Now that you've said what you had to say, it's my turn to inform you of a few things. I am sorry Glen filled your head with such nonsense. I am not interested in your husband, never was and never will be. I feel so sorry for you and your children. He has deceived you greatly. I really regret telling you this, but, you married a rapist."

I didn't give her a chance to respond. I hung up the phone. A few minutes later, I heard my mother coming up the stairs to talk to me. She was still upset over the phone call I received.

"Don't worry about her, mom. I told her a truth she didn't know, whether she believed it or not, it doesn't matter. It had to be done."

"What are you talking about, Gerri?" she asked.

"Not now, mom, not now."

CHAPTER 3

It was mid-February when I received a call from one of my friends in the neighborhood.

"Did you see the paper today?" she asked.

"No, I didn't, why?" I questioned.

"Go and buy a paper right now. There's an article about a rape of a white woman which took place in the neighborhood and Glen is in the story," she related.

"Okay, I'll talk to you later."

I hurriedly hung up the phone, hurried to the store and purchased a paper. When I returned home, I sat at the bottom of the stairs and began to read. The article was several pages long.

It dealt with fear more so than just the act of rape. The woman described her attacker as six feet tall. Immediately I dispelled any thoughts that it could have been Glen until I got to the end of the article. It read that Glen was a suspect in the incident.

Somehow, I wasn't really surprised. I reread the story over several times. I felt so bad for this woman. Then I realized this rape could have been prevented. Tears welled up in my eyes. I felt responsible for what had happened to her. If I had reported my rape maybe he wouldn't have been walking the streets. Here was a woman who wasn't afraid to stand up to him. I envied her courage. I was the coward. My own fears engulfed me and I felt helpless to do anything. The guilt stayed with me for many months. I repeated in my mind over and over, I could have saved her, but I didn't. The burden was so heavy to bear. Every time I thought of that woman, I cried.

The next time Glen showed up at my house uninvited, I told him about the newspaper article.

"Let me see the paper, he requested.

I gave it to him. He glanced over it.

"This isn't true. I want to borrow this. I will bring it back," he told me.

I never saw that paper again, even though I asked him for it several times. He disappeared along with the paper.

In my sixth month of pregnancy I was shoved into a wall by students running from a bat. Others were falling over one another trying to get out of the path of the flying mammal. Often, fights broke out during class changes and the hallways weren't safe. The school administrator removed all the pregnant girls and sent us to a building housed for unwed mothers. The teachers sent over our assignments each week and we had to complete our work in order to graduate. Those who lived at the unwed home were planning to give their babies up for adoption, while others like myself, were just there to finish the high school term.

Two months later I had a doctor's appointment with my gynecologist. Just as I was leaving the office, Glen showed up.

"How did you know where to find me?" I asked.

"Mrs. Wilkins told me you were here," he answered.

Mrs. Wilkins was the elderly lady who lived on the third floor in my house.

"Well, she shouldn't have said anything," I snapped.

"Come on. You shouldn't be traveling around on public transportation, alone," Glen replied.

"I'm pregnant, not sick."

"Get in the car. I'm taking you home," he demanded.

I became irritated. His constant badgering was extremely annoying.

Glen got behind the wheel. He drove down the expressway. As we neared Dee-Dee's neighborhood, he headed off the exit and hit the accelerator. Glen was speeding down the ramp at 100 mph.

"What is wrong with you? Are you trying to kill me and my baby? Slow down now," I screamed.

I clutched the side of the door handle, my eyes bulging with fear as he laughed hysterically.

"It's not funny, Glen. You're crazy," I screamed as he reduced the speed of the car back down to the normal speed limit. When he parked the car in front of my house, I got out.

"Stay away from me Glen. I mean it."

I was eight months pregnant and my life could have ended that day.

I prayed often, especially about the horrible things Glen did to me. I participated in my church functions as often as I could. One day the pastor confronted me and said that I shouldn't make myself too prominent around the church. His words cut deep. If God didn't want me in His church He would've put me out. I certainly wasn't going to let man do so.

I asked my mother to go shopping with me so that I could find a nice dress to wear to church on Easter Sunday. When Easter arrived, I proudly walked into church boldly displaying my belly in my new outfit and didn't really care what people thought. I had every right to be there, just like them.

On May 12, 1972 at 6:00 a.m., I felt my first labor pain. I laid in my bed, not sure of what was going to happen next. At 6:30 a.m. the second pain hit. I didn't say anything to my mother. She was getting ready for work and I didn't want her to stay home with me. At 9:00 a.m., I decided to let her know what was happening.

"How long have you been having these pains?" she asked.

"About every half hour since early this morning," I replied.

"Why didn't you let me know? Do you want me to stay home and go to the hospital with you?"

"No mom. I'll be all right. I can get there on my own. Please go to work. If I need you I will call you," I assured her.

"Okay, but don't stay here too long. I will check back with you in a little while," she added.

"Relax mom, I heard that the first baby always take a while to get here. I promise I will leave soon. Please don't worry," I said.

I sat down on the bottom step as I watched my mother leave the house. I glanced at my watch. It was 9:05 a.m. At ten o'clock I called for a cab. The pains were now fifteen minutes apart. As soon as I hung up the phone, it rang. My mother was on the other end of the line.

"Why are you still at home?" Please call a cab and go to the hospital," she pleaded.

"I did, mom. The cab is on the way. I will see you this evening. Stop worrying. I will be all right," I assured her.

The cab pulled up outside. He blew the horn announcing his arrival.

Another pain hit me as I tried to get up from the step. When it had subsided, I walked to the door with my overnight bag. The cab driver looked at me questionably.

"Are you alright, Miss?" he asked.

"Yes, I'm fine. Take me to Germantown Hospital, please."

I didn't give any sign that I was in a hurry, though I looked as if I would give birth at any moment. The look on the cabby's face revealed, please don't have this baby in my cab.

I got in the back seat. The cabby placed my bag inside on the floor. When I arrived at the hospital, I got out of the cab. The driver walked around to help me with my bag. As he pulled away from the curb, I headed toward the front entrance. Another pain hit me as I reached for the door.

Once inside the hospital, I walked around for several minutes, as if lost, wondering which way to go. Finally a staff person walked up to me.

"Are you being admitted?" she asked.

"Yes," I replied.

She directed me to where I needed to go. The nurses started to prep me for examination. I looked around but I didn't see my intern there. I inquired as to his whereabouts. They told me they would try to get in touch with him. Two or three doctors came to check on me. At some point in time one of them decided that I may not be ready just yet and was considering sending me back home. That didn't make sense to me because my pains were now ten minutes apart. On further examination it was determined that I would stay. I walked around a lot that day. Shortly after 5 p.m. my baby was born. My intern never showed up. Once again I inquired about him.

"We've been trying to locate him all day but we can't find him," the nurse said.

"He's going to be very disappointed that he missed the birth," I replied.

My mother arrived at the hospital around six o'clock.

"Are you okay?" she asked.

"Yes, mom, I'm fine. I'm numb so I'm not in pain."

My mother walked to the nursery. When she returned she said, "she's beautiful, Gerri."

I nodded my head in agreement.

"Mom, do not let Glen know I'm here if he inquires. I don't want him here."

"You know I won't tell him," she replied.

My mother stayed with me for an hour.

"I'll see you tomorrow," she promised.

Later that evening I informed the staff on the maternity ward that I didn't want any visitors except my mother. I didn't call any of my friends to let them know I had given birth.

Early the next morning, my intern showed up.

"I'm sorry I wasn't here. I was in class and no one called me," he apologized.

"I'm sorry you weren't here too but they told me they couldn't locate you. It's a shame no one thought of calling the school."

I could see the disappointment in his face. It was part of his training to witness the birth process, but I told him he would get another opportunity. After chatting with me for a few minutes he left.

I wanted to bond with my baby so I attempted to breast feed. I lasted two days. I was in so much pain that I couldn't feed her and I developed a fever. On the third day, the nurse rolled a breast pump machine into my room.

"You are accumulating too much milk which is causing your fever. You have to pump out a jar of milk every evening. You can't breast feed while having a fever. We will give your baby a bottle," she said.

I wanted to breast feed my baby but I couldn't adapt. My nipples were red like strawberries and I was too sore. I shed many tears because of it. The next day they brought her to me and handed me a bottle to feed her. I looked into my baby's eyes as she sucked down the formula, her little tiny fingers wrapped around mine. Her dark, beautiful eyes were so penetrating that it seemed as if she was staring through to the depths of my soul. It frightened me and I was afraid I might drop her, but actually she was very secure in my arms. She was one of the most beautiful babies I have ever seen and she was mine.

That evening I was lying in bed when suddenly I was aware of someone watching me. I looked up to see Glen standing in the doorway, dressed in army fatigue. I became very agitated.

"What are you doing here, Glen? I told the staff you weren't allowed in here. Get out of here," I ordered. "How did you know I was here?"

"Mrs. Wilkins told me," he grinned impishly.

She tried to find out things about me so she could tell him. She thought I treated Glen very unfairly, but then again, she didn't know the whole story. I refused to talk to her about him. She befriended him, unaware of his manipulative nature. Unknowingly, she became his only source for information.

He looked at me with a smirk on his face, nodding his head for several seconds. Then he turned and walked away. For some reason I didn't believe he was taking the next elevator down. I forced myself to climb out of bed, knowing I had a fever and not feeling well. I slowly made my way to the nursery where I found Glen staring at the baby. He had the nurse to move the baby closer so he could get a better look. Glen continued to stare at her for several minutes. Without looking at me he began to speak.

"That is not my baby. She doesn't look anything like me," he retorted.

He repeated it over and over again several times.

"You're right about one thing. She is not your baby. She is my baby," I said emphatically.

I turned and walked away. When I looked back, I saw Glen push the button for the elevator.

On the evening of the fifth day, the doctor came to visit me. He told me I couldn't be released with a fever. I waited for the change in shift. When the night nurses came on, I pumped so much milk out that I was certain my fever would break by morning. It was midnight. The sound of the suction cup pumping milk could be heard from the hallway. One of the nurses peered in to see what I was doing. I looked up at her but said nothing. She didn't say anything either. I was sweating and I felt very warm. Next, I went to the window and threw it up as high as I could. A beautiful, comfortable breeze blew through the opened window. I climbed back in bed and I said to myself aloud, "I am going home tomorrow."

When the doctor made his rounds the next morning he came in reading his chart.

"You can't go home today, Miss Tate. You still have a fever," he said.

"I feel just fine Doc. Take my temperature," I requested.

"We'll see. If your fever is gone when the nurse checks it, you can go home."

Hours later, I left the hospital. After six days in the hospital, I arrived home with my baby in my arms. I stepped out of the cab, alongside my mother and I slowly ascended the steps to the front porch. I leaned into the hedges as I tried to regain my balance.

"Take the baby, mom," as I reached over to hand her Janel.

Arms outstretched, my mother took the baby and I grabbed the handrail to steady myself.

"Are you okay?" she asked.

"I'm a little dizzy, that's all," I replied.

"Please be careful! Don't fall!" she cried.

I glanced across the street to see Sidney's mother standing in her doorway, something she often did. I continued up the steps and into the house. Once inside my room I climbed into bed. My mother laid my little bundle of joy down in her bassinet next to me. She was sound asleep. I was weak and needed a lot of rest, so my mom tended to the baby.

A half hour later the doorbell rang. I heard my mother talking to someone downstairs.

"Gerri, you have a visitor," my mom yelled.

Minutes later Sidney's mother appeared in the doorway.

"How are you feeling, Gerri? I saw you when you came home a while ago."

"I'm okay, just tired," I replied.

She walked over to the bassinet and peered in.

"Is it alright if I pick her up?" she inquired.

"Sure, you can," I replied.

She held the baby for a long time, talking and staring at her. I had to wonder if she thought Sidney was the father. She may have had her suspicions but if so, she didn't indicate it.

A month passed. It was time for graduation. I lost interest in preparing for the ceremony. All I wanted was a diploma. My mother was looking forward to seeing me march down the aisle in a cap and gown. I was more interested in taking care of Janel. When I told my mother I was thinking of not attending the graduation ceremony, she seemed disappointed.

"Maybe Glen will watch the baby for a few hours."

I looked at her like she was crazy. Then I remembered. Because of my secrets, she doesn't know about the rotten things he has done.

"I don't know, mom. I don't trust him like that," I said.

When Glen showed up a few days later, my mother took it upon herself to ask Glen to babysit while we go to the graduation.

"I'll watch her," he agreed.

I really didn't want to deprive my mother of watching her only daughter graduate from high school, so I agreed.

After the ceremony, we returned home. When I entered my room I found Glen asleep on my bed. I didn't see Janel anywhere. She wasn't in her bassinet.

"Glen, wake up. Where is my baby?" I shouted.

"She's right here. Stop hollering." He lifted his arm. Nestled under his armpit was Janel.

"Are you crazy? You could've smothered my baby. You don't fall asleep with a baby lying under your arms," I screamed.

I picked my baby up and she started to stir.

"My God, what were you thinking?"

I turned to Glen.

"You can leave now."

"As you can see, the baby is fine. I would never hurt her."

"Well, I don't know about that. She has a bassinet. You should've put her in it, not under your armpit."

I was so disgusted. I cradled Janel in my arms for several minutes before placing her back in her bed. Glen left the house after apologizing for the mishap. I didn't see much of Glen after that. His visits became very sporadic over the next few months. On one occasion he bought her two cans of formula. I'm surprised he bought her anything considering his denial of paternity. When he appeared, he paid very little attention to the baby. He would glance at her from time to time when he thought I wasn't looking. Each time he entered my house I couldn't wait for him to leave.

One day Janel was constantly crying for more than an hour. I picked her up and checked her diaper. She was dry. I shoved a bottle between her lips. She didn't want it. I rocked her, but to no avail. I walked around the room with her. She screamed louder and louder. I needed help with her. My mother wasn't home. My nerves were frayed and I lost patience with her. I laid her on her back. She screamed. I turned her on her stomach. She screamed. Nothing I did seem to satisfy her. Finally I just lost it and in my depressive state of mind, I slapped her on her bottom. She screamed even louder. In that moment I realized what I had done. It wasn't her fault that I was a livid mess. I picked up my baby and quickly ran my hand over her bottom, comforting her. I talked to her lovingly, apologizing to my sweet, precious baby for my temperament. I hugged and kissed her face and lips while holding her close to my bosom. The love that flowed from me to her was enough to soothe my beautiful baby. I vowed never to get that upset again. She nestled her little head and fingers in my chest and before I knew it, all the screaming had subsided. My little baby let me know that she could trust me to keep her safe. She went to sleep in my arms and I returned her to her bassinet. I stroked her hair as she settled in. How beautiful she was, as I watched her sleep. From that day forward, I vowed that my daughter would not pay the price for the pain Glen had inflicted on me. This small, innocent baby was my whole life.

Several weeks later Glen's mother called to inform me that he had been arrested. He was charged with the rape incident when the victim positively identified him. At his trial he was tried and convicted. He received a sentence of ten to twenty years. I was jubilant. Finally, he was out of my life. It was my time to celebrate.

Not long after, Sidney came home on leave for a brief period. Someone informed him about Janel. He showed up on my doorstep. I held the door open for him to enter.

"I can't turn my back for a minute before you end up messing around with somebody else."

I stared at him in disbelief.

"You shouldn't have said that to me. You know better than that."

"Well, what do you expect me to say?"

"You know what Sidney? It doesn't really matter anymore. See you later."

Sidney let himself out. After all I had invested in our relationship, he perceived me as unfaithful. I was deeply hurt by his accusation. He didn't need to know what happened. It no longer mattered. I lost all respect for him, just as he had for me, the day I lost my virginity. Devastated as I was, I knew I had to move on. Heartbroken and sad for a long time, the emotional pain eventually eased.

CHAPTER 4

EIGHTEEN MONTHS PASSED SINCE THAT fateful encounter with Glen. Bad thoughts and fear constantly plagued me. Life was looking pretty bleak now. The one constant in my life was my beautiful baby girl. I sat straddle-legged on the floor opposite Janel. I adored watching her discover new things like crawling, walking and playing with her toys. She brightened my days when moments of sadness would set in. I had an outlet, an escape from the hard reality of what I faced day in and day out. I raised my head in time to see my mother enter the room.

"Why don't you look for a job, Gerri? You have completed your computer training and I think a job may help take your mind off things," she suggested.

I nodded in agreement.

"You're right, mom. I need to look for work. You know I appreciate all that you do but I want to buy Janel's diapers and formula, after all she is my responsibility."

"Please don't feel that I am pushing you to contribute financially. We are going to be all right."

"I know mom," I replied.

I watched my mother as she gently picked the baby up, planting a kiss on her forehead. I knew money was very tight in our household and it really was a strain on my mother to meet the bills with an extra mouth to feed. I stretched out my hands to take Janel as mom turned to leave. I placed Janel back on the floor, reached for her piano and set it in front of her. Her tiny fingers banged on the keys. I started to laugh. She looked up as if to say, "See mommy?"

Three weeks later I landed my first job working for an assurance company as a keypunch operator. I was very excited about it, but shortly after starting work I became ill. It was very cold in the office. The air-conditioning unit was turned up so high as to prevent the machines from overheating. I wasn't accustomed to air-conditioned rooms, which may have contributed to my illness. It's just a bad cold, I thought. I didn't give it a second thought until I realized some of the symptoms weren't going away.

In the weeks that followed, I continued to deteriorate. Every day became a nightmare. My heartbeat was very rapid. I felt dizzy after each episode. I had to hold my breath to slow down and stop the rapid heartbeats. The suffocating feeling I experienced forced me to breathe through my mouth. These symptoms alone occurred several times a day. The only relief I had was at night when I laid flat on my back in bed or on the floor. The left side of my neck had a pea-sized knot that grew larger and larger as the weeks passed. My energy level was practically zero. I pushed myself to do my everyday tasks. On several occasions, my mother had to take over the care of Janel. Some days were worse than others. It was very frightening. I couldn't go to work on most days.

I was on the job approximately two weeks when I became ill. I was afraid I would lose my job. After so many call-outs, my supervisor became alarmed. She asked me to come into the office as soon as I could. They were impressed with my job performance. I hoped that it would be sufficient to maintain my position with the company.

The next good day I had, I went to the office. I obtained a note from my doctor showing the period of time I had been under his care. My supervisor and co-workers looked up at me as I entered. They were glad to see me. Some thought I had quit my job. I stood next to my supervisor and she scrutinized me very carefully. She could see how sick I was. I tried to turn my head and couldn't. Then she noticed the knot on my neck. It was almost like she pitied me. The good news was, she would hold my job for me. I was asked to come to work on days when I felt well enough to do so. The visit to the office was well worth it. I wanted them to see for themselves how ill I really was. I was blessed that they didn't fire me. I really needed this job so that I could take care of Janel properly. That evening, I prayed to God, giving thanks for keeping me gainfully employed.

There was a family doctor who had an office up the street from my house. He was very loved by his patients. He was old-fashioned in his technique at times but he catered to everyone's budget. The home remedies he suggested were better than the prescribed medications in my opinion. I trusted this doctor because he was so knowledgeable and he showed a genuine interest in his patients. I believed, if anyone could diagnose my problem, he would be the one. From the onset of my illness, I faithfully followed his instructions.

One day I was walking up the street for my regularly scheduled doctor's appointment when I ran into one of my best friends.

"Hi Margie," I greeted. "Are you ready for your big day?" I asked.

"Well, hello there and how are you doing, Gerri?" she chuckled. Suddenly, she moved closer to me to get a better look.

"Hey, you don't look so well. Are you okay?" Margie asked with a look of concern that covered her face.

"No, I am not well," I replied. "I have been sick for over two months and I'm on my way to pay my doctor a visit.

"Oh my, I'm sorry to hear that! No wonder I haven't heard from you lately. Well, do you think you will be able to attend my nuptials on Saturday?" she asked.

"Are you kidding? I wouldn't dream of missing the event of the century for anything in the world. I will be there with bells on."

I tried desperately to muster a laugh but the lump protruding from my neck made it almost impossible. My lymph nodes were very swollen.

"Well, take care of yourself and I really hope you can make it on Saturday," Margie said.

"Okay, see you then," I replied.

We bid each other farewell and continued on our separate ways.

Saturday came and I prepared to go to the wedding. I felt awful but I had promised Margie that I wouldn't miss her wedding for anything. I forced my legs to carry me to the church. After the ceremony concluded, I anxiously waited to receive the bride and groom in the vestibule once they exited the sanctuary.

"Margie," I called out. "Congratulations! You look beautiful. I'm sorry I can't stay for the reception. I must go and see my doctor immediately. I feel very weak."

I reached out to hug and kiss my friend.

"May God bless you both on your marriage and have a nice reception. I will see you soon."

"Thank you Gerri, for being here for me. You will get better soon. I just know it," Margie assured me.

She watched me leave the church through the beautiful red doors.

As I ran down the steps, I thought about how happy Margie was. Tears streamed down my face as I hurriedly walked to the avenue to take the trolley. Would I live long enough to experience the joy of getting married someday? I had been ill for almost three months and I wondered if I would ever recover.

Later at the doctor's office I sat waiting for Dr. Zeldin to admit me inside the inner office. He appeared almost immediately to let me in even though it seemed like hours. He pulled out my chart and stared at it for several minutes before commenting.

My hope of ever recovering started to fade as I watched intently the grim expression on his face. This is it. The doctor has bad news for me. I am going to die and no one seems to know what's wrong with me, I thought to myself.

Finally, the doctor leaned forward and scratched his head with perplexity. He muttered something inaudible as he examined the swollen gland still enlarged on my neck.

"I have tested you for just about everything imaginable in this case: Tonsillitis, Mononucleosis, non-Hodgkin's lymphoma and Leukemia, and yet, each test has come back negative. Your white cell count is only slightly elevated; not enough to indicate any serious infection. I have given you every antibiotic I can think of. I don't understand what's causing these symptoms, so I'll be consulting a specialist next week to examine you if there isn't any improvement. I don't want to alarm you," he said. "In the meantime, continue to take the medicine I prescribed for you."

I felt I had a lot to worry about as I left the doctor's office and walked towards home. I was very afraid and uncertainty raced through my mind. As I walked down the street, I noticed a small statured woman with a lot of spunk, standing on her porch. It was my second mom, Ellen Phillips, a woman who took a liking to me, and treated me as if I were one of her own daughters.

"Hi dear," she greeted, as I drew near. "You don't feel well, do you?" she asked.

"No," I replied.

"Fred and I are on our way to church service. Please come along and go with us this evening," Mrs. Phillips pleaded.

"That sounds very nice," I responded, "but I don't think I can make it. All of my strength is gone and I feel very weak." I replied.

Oh, come on," Ellen urged. "Please let us try to help you. We want to pray a special prayer over you. It will only take a few minutes for you to get ready. Don't rush. You have enough time. We will wait for you," she promised as she turned to enter the house.

"Well, all right. I will go," I agreed hesitantly. "I will need about fifteen minutes or so to get ready, then I shall return."

I moved rather slowly as I headed for home. A short while later I returned to find my neighbors standing on the sidewalk. Fred helped me get into the car. I leaned back against the seat. A few minutes later I lowered the window to breathe in some fresh air. A suffocating feeling overwhelmed me, something I had experienced on many occasions in the past two and a half months.

There were several people in the church when we arrived, all suffering from one ailment or another. We found seats and sat down. I looked around nervously and listened to the bishop as he spoke over the people with their various disabilities and hardships. The service was very uplifting and near the end, the bishop had everyone to form a circle as he sent out special blessings for each of the afflicted. Next, he requested a line formation. In his right hand he held a large stone which he referred to as the "Rock of Jerusalem" and lightly touched it to the forehead of each person as they passed by him. I watched in bewilderment. Will this rock make me well again? I wondered as I approached him. The bishop gently clutched my arm and held it firmly as he placed the rock to my forehead. As Bishop Steel prayed, my body started to tremble. Tears rushed to my eyes as I stood there, completely baffled, perspiration dripping from my face and neck. When the Phillips saw what was happening they rushed to my side and led me back to my seat. I watched as the bishop continued to place the rock on each person as they passed by him. None of the others had the type of reaction I did. I asked myself, "What is wrong with me?"

When the service was over, I noticed Bishop Steel and the Phillips huddled to one side of the room speaking in low voices. Every once in a while they glanced over at me. I was sure they were conferring about me. The trip home was spent in almost total silence.

The next day, I stopped by the Phillips home. As I entered the house, I was met by Ellen, who quickly took me aside. A sad expression came over the woman as she stared at me.

"What's wrong, Mrs. Phillips?" I inquired. "It's me, isn't it? You are worried about me."

"Honey, bishop wants to see you at a private meeting at four o'clock next Sunday. Please allow me to take you," Ellen begged.

"Why not, what do I have to lose?"

"I have always said, you are like my own daughter and I hate seeing you like this."

Mrs. Phillips embraced me and held me to her bosom as a tear dropped from my eyelid.

On Sunday afternoon, I went with Mrs. Phillips to the house where the private gathering was held. When we entered, we discovered about seven people ahead of us. Ellen turned to me.

"You must wait your turn," she said.

"Okay, I replied."

As the minutes dragged on, the suffocating feeling returned and I became very pale. Three ladies seated on the sofa immediately vacated their seats so that I could have full use of the sofa. I slumped down onto the sofa with Mrs. Phillips seated next to me. The ladies who accommodated us were chatting with Ellen.

"She is very ill, we can see that."

Ellen nodded her head in agreement.

"It's all right to let her see bishop next. We don't mind waiting a little longer," said one of the women.

"Thank you all for being so kind," replied Ellen.

A few minutes had passed but it seemed like an eternity.

"Come on, Gerri. It's your turn."

Ellen nudged me gently as I opened my eyes. She helped me up from the sofa.

"Are you okay?" she asked.

"Yes, I think so," I replied.

"Bishop is straight through that door," pointing the way to the kitchen.

"Do you want some help, dear?" Ellen asked.

"No thank you. I think I can make it."

I walked to the kitchen and stood in the doorway.

Bishop Steel sat at the head of the table, his hands resting on a bible in front of him. His head was lowered, as if in deep meditation. For several seconds neither of us spoke. Finally, he looked up, his deep penetrating eyes piercing me like a sword. He beckoned for me to enter and have a seat. I pulled the chair out from the table and sat down. After what seemed like several minutes, he finally spoke.

"Is there anything you wish to tell me?" he asked.

"Where should I begin?" I inquired.

"Wherever you want to," he replied.

I began to speak of my symptoms that I was experiencing, the rapid heart palpitations and the suffocating feeling that recurred several times a day. I talked about the knot on my neck and how I couldn't turn my head from side to side. After I had finished speaking, he stared at me for several seconds before speaking.

"Someone in your life is trying to destroy you."

Immediately I thought of Glen. I sat there speechless. How could he know that? The Phillips couldn't have told him. They didn't know anything about Glen other than the fact he was Janel's father. This whole meeting was beginning to frighten me. I didn't know what to make of it.

"This is what I want you to do."

He reached into his pocket and pulled out some items.

"I'm going to give you this cloth."

He held a black and gold satin, triangular cloth in one hand, in the other, a miniature bottle of oil with herbs.

"Soak it with the oil and wear it next to your heart, for it will slow down your heartbeats. Place a glass of red wine on Psalm 35 for one hour at the exact same hour each day. Read the passage and drink the wine. Do this for seven days."

He picked up another bottle from the table. It contained granules that looked like bath beads.

"On the seventh day, pour this entire bottle into your bath water and soak in the tub for exactly twenty minutes. Do you understand the instructions?" he asked.

"Yes," I replied, nodding my head.

I picked up everything he gave me and quickly left the room.

Mrs. Phillips was waiting for me in the living room. She was still chatting with the women when I returned.

"Are you okay, Gerri?" she asked.

"Yes, I have some things Bishop Steel instructed me to do."

We left the house and headed back home.

The next day when my heart palpitations began, I poured some oil on the satin cloth and placed it inside my bra, next to my heart. The heart beats slowed. I decided I would wear the cloth all day long when I was out. At home I would wear it when it was absolutely necessary. I felt better since wearing the cloth. There was a drastic difference in my symptoms. I could breathe better and that was a plus after weeks of gasping for air.

There were times when I had to sit on steps of storefronts, waiting for the trolley, whenever I got dizzy. Another time, I fell backwards off a bar stool in a restaurant. Young men playing the ping pong machine ran over to catch me before I hit the floor. Those were very unpredictable moments for me, therefore, I stayed away from my friends. I didn't want to subject them to my illness.

On my way home, I had a friend stop at the State Store to purchase a bottle of red wine for me. When I got home I placed the bottle of wine on the dresser. I began setting up my things for the seven-day ritual as the bishop instructed. I pulled my vanity stool over next to my bed and sat the bible on top. I opened the book to Psalm 35. Next I got a six ounce juice glass from the kitchen. I poured the wine into the glass and sat it atop the 35th Psalm. I glanced at my watch. It was four o'clock in the afternoon. It had to sit there for one hour. At 5:00 p.m., I returned to my room. I picked up the bible and began to read aloud Psalm 35:

"Plead my cause, O Lord, with them that strive with me: fight against them that fight against me. 2 Take hold of shield and buckler, and stand up for mine help. 3 Draw out also the spear, and stop the way against them that persecute me: say unto my soul, I am thy salvation. 4 Let them be confounded and put to shame that seek after my soul: let them be turned back and brought to confusion that devise my hurt. 5 Let them be as chaff before the wind: and let the angel of the Lord chase them. 6 Let their way be dark and slippery: and let the angel of the Lord persecute them. 7 For without cause have they hid for me their net in a pit, which without cause they have digged for my soul. 8 Let destruction come upon him at unawares; and let his net that he hath hid catch himself: into that very destruction let him fall. 9 And my soul shall be joyful in the Lord: it shall rejoice in his salvation. 10 All my bones shall say, Lord, who is like unto thee, which deliverest the poor from him that is too strong for him, yea, the poor and the needy from him that spoileth him? 11 False witnesses did rise up; they laid to my charge things that I knew not. 12 They rewarded me evil for good to the spoiling of my soul. 13 But as for me, when they were sick, my clothing was sackcloth: I humbled my soul with fasting; and my prayer returned into mine own bosom. 14 I behaved myself as though he had been my friend or brother: I bowed down heavily, as one that mourneth for his mother. 15 But in mine adversity they rejoiced, and gathered themselves together: yea, the abjects gathered themselves together against me, and I knew it not; they did tear me, and ceased not: 16 With hypocritical mockers in feasts, they gnashed upon me with their teeth. 17 Lord, how long wilt thou look on? rescue my soul from their destructions, my darling from the lions. 18 I will give thee thanks in the great congregation: I will praise thee among much people. 19 Let not them that are mine enemies wrongfully rejoice over me: neither let them wink with the eye that hate me without a cause. 20 For they speak not peace: but they devise deceitful matters against them that are quiet in the land. 21 Yea, they opened their mouth wide against me, and said, Aha, aha, our eye hath seen it. 22 This thou hast seen, O Lord; keep not silence: O Lord, be not far from me. 23 Stir up thyself, and awake to my judgment, even unto my cause, my God and my Lord. 24 Judge me, O Lord my God, according to thy righteousness; and let them not rejoice over me. 25 Let them not say in their hearts, Ah, so would we have it: let them not say, We have swallowed him up. 26 Let them be ashamed and brought to confusion together that rejoice at mine hurt: let them be clothed with shame and dishonour that magnify themselves against me. 27 Let them shout for joy, and be glad, that favour my righteous cause: yea, let them say continually, Let the Lord be magnified, which hath pleasure in the prosperity of his servant. 28 And my tongue shall speak of thy righteousness and of thy praise all the day long."

Then I drank the wine.

I thought about all I had been through. I was getting tired of the uphill battle I constantly faced every day. I realize that every human being has their cross to bear. Evidently, this was mine. I prayed many days and nights. I asked myself, does God really hear me? Of course He does, everything in His time, not mine. If I should die, I didn't want Glen to try and seek custody of Janel, even though he denied paternity at birth. I felt I had to protect my daughter, no matter what. She was my lifeline. As I peered over at my beautiful daughter, every part of my being said fight, fight for your life and hers. You have everything to live for. I believed it. At that moment, I realized this wasn't something normal happening to me. It wasn't an ordinary illness. It was baffling, even to my doctor. I was dealing with something unimaginable. My thoughts drifted back to all the mind-boggling things Glen did to me throughout my pregnancy. I wasn't just dealing with a guy who made bad decisions. I was fighting Satan himself.

For seven days I followed meticulously the instructions given me by the bishop. But on the seventh day I came through my front door, very weak. I could hardly breathe. I felt my life being sucked from my body. My mother looked at me.

"You look awful, Gerri. What's wrong?' she asked.

"Mom, I followed all the instructions. I was feeling better these past few days and now I feel so bad again."

I hurried past my mother and climbed the stairs. I began to think that everything I had done, thus far, was in vain. The suffocating feeling returned, as well as the heart palpitations. I became very discouraged. Hurrying to my room, I grabbed a glass and poured the wine quickly, placing it on Psalm 35. I looked at my watch. It was 4:00 p.m. I was just in time. The hour wait seemed like it would never come. I was desperate. I couldn't understand how everything was coming unraveled. I doused the satin cloth with oil and placed it next to my heart. I tried to wait patiently. At 5:00 p.m. I read the 35th Psalm, and I drank the wine. Next, I picked up the bottle of bath beads. I ran the water in the bathtub and emptied the entire bottle of beads into the water. The beads emitted a sweet aroma as it mixed with the running water. I laid my watch on the edge of the tub where it rested against the wall. I needed to keep track of the time. I gently lowered myself in the water and started to relax. Ten minutes went by. The aroma from the beads overtook me. I couldn't breathe. I became very agitated. I needed to get out. Each time I tried to escape from the fumes, an unknown force held me by my ankle, like an undercurrent wave in an ocean. I looked down at my ankle. The stopper was securely covering the drain. Oh my God, I thought. I can't take this. I finally stopped fighting and rested my head against the back of the tub. I glanced at the time. Just ten more minutes to go, then I can get out, I thought to myself. I closed my eyes as I waited. When I opened my eyes again, exactly ten minutes had elapsed. I raised myself slowly; nothing tugged at my ankle to keep me there. Everything was peaceful. I climbed out and toweled myself dry. I walked across the room. I couldn't feel my feet touching the floor. I felt as if I were literally walking on air. I looked down. I could clearly see that my feet were firmly planted on the floor. I stood in front of the mirror. The huge knot on my neck had been reduced to almost nothing. I turned my head from left to right. The stiffness was gone. A renewed strength took over. I was rejuvenated. I no longer felt ill. It was the best moment of my life since the onset of my illness. My face glowed with a new radiance. As I left the bathroom, my mom came up the stairs.

"Gerri, you look so much better. What happened?" she asked.

"Mom, I feel like I don't have a care in the world. Nothing bothers me anymore. I feel like a brand new me," I replied.

I went to my doctor's office the following day with a new confidence. I knew deep down inside, there wasn't any need to see a specialist, but the doctor had summoned me. He examined my neck and shook his head, speechless almost.

"The lump in your neck is practically gone. How can that be?" he wondered.

"I don't know Doc, but I have truly been blessed."

A week later I was seated at Ellen's table having lunch. We were conversing about the events of the past three months.

"I want to know why you looked at me with such a sad expression in your eyes the night of the prayer service," I asked.

"Well, honey," she paused. "Bishop Steel told Fred and I your survival depended on the strength of your own faith, otherwise, you would have been dead in maybe two weeks' time. I couldn't tell you then because I didn't want to frighten you and cause you to lose faith. I wanted you to fight to live and conquer this illness that has plagued you for so long," she answered. "After all, I've always said, you are like one of my own daughters," she added, and I love you."

CHAPTER 5

It was May, 1974. Janel just turned two years old. I was visiting Dee-Dee. I brought Janel with me because she hadn't seen her for quite a while. I sat on her porch, Janel fast asleep, face down on my lap. A young man passed by and spoke to me. I returned the greeting. I noticed he entered the house two doors up from Dee-Dee's. A half hour later he came out of the house and walked up Dee-Dee's steps and introduced himself.

"Hi, I'm Daniel," he said.

"Hello, Daniel, how are you?" I asked. "I'm Gerri."

"Is this your baby?" peering at Janel. She's cute."

"Yes, she is, thank you," I replied.

We talked for a long time. From that day forward, we agreed to get better acquainted, even though I wasn't really ready for a new relationship after the damage Glen had inflicted on me. Daniel was a handsome, nice quiet gentleman and I liked him a lot.

Four weeks after we met, he bought a Polaroid SX-70 camera for my birthday. He was a very generous gift giver.

Three months into the courtship, Daniel proposed.

"Daniel, we need to talk about this first. There are some things you need to know about me."

"Okay, I'm all ears," he replied.

"We'll discuss this tomorrow." It's getting late and I need to think a few things through."

Once alone in my room, I weighed my options. I thought of all the reasons why I should get married, then I thought of all the reasons why I shouldn't.

When Glen was arrested, I celebrated his incarceration. I thought he was out of my life for good but he found new ways to interfere. He used Mrs. Wilkins as his vehicle of communication. I saw her sitting on the porch one day reading a letter from him. Over the months there were many letters coming on a regular basis. I thought to myself, so that's how he's been finding out things about me. From then on, I had to be very cautious about what I said in her presence. I also informed my mother about the letters so she wouldn't voluntarily share any information that I didn't want divulged. Glen's persistence in finding out what was going on in my household greatly disturbed me. I wanted to be rid of him once and for all. Second, I didn't want his influence in my child's development, whatsoever. I was ready to change my name and address.

There were times when Glen had his mother to call me. She wanted to take Janel to the prison to see him. I knew it was his idea.

"No, I don't want my baby in that environment," I told her.

She pleaded with me to change my mind. His mother was a nice lady, unlike her son, and I felt bad for her. She showed great interest in the child, much more than Glen.

Finally I agreed to accompany her on one of her visits but I made it quite clear that this wasn't going to become a habit.

On the other hand, I didn't feel that Daniel and I had known each other long enough to consider marriage. I had too many issues to deal with and I didn't want to drag all this baggage into a new relationship. Even though I cared for Daniel very much, I didn't think this type of love constituted the basis for marriage, however, I left room for the fact that true love could grow.

I tossed and turned all night. When morning broke, I was very tired. I grabbed a cup of coffee, lit a cigarette and put on my thinking cap. I often smoked, particularly whenever I had big decisions to make. It helped clear my head, even though I knew smoking was very unhealthy. One day I would probably try to quit, that is, whenever life would be kinder to me. After weighing everything carefully, I decided to marry Daniel.

Later in the day, I sat Daniel down and started revealing some of the things he needed to know before he got overexcited about marriage. I explained all that I had been through with Glen and how I felt I was emotionally unprepared to be that woman he would need as a spouse. When I had finished telling him the story I asked him a few questions.

"It will take a very understanding individual to deal with the issues that I have. Do you believe that you are ready to commit to that?"

"Yes, I believe I can handle it, Gerri. We can work on those issues together," he answered.

"In that case, I say yes, to your proposal."

Days later, Daniel and I started the wedding preparations. I wanted a real wedding ceremony. I thought about Margie and how happy she was the day she married. I remembered thinking, would I ever live to see my own wedding day. I jumped at the opportunity of becoming a bride. I was excited. Like all brides, I wanted everything to be perfect on that day.

My sister-in-law, Mary offered to make my wedding gown. I was so excited. I chose white velvet fabric and she suggested sewing seed pearls around the neck, sleeves and bodice of the gown. When the gown was completed, I tried it on for size. It fit perfectly and it was so beautiful. I had a gown like no other, plain, yet simple. The pearls enhanced it so much that it accented the gown to perfection. My attendants' gowns were made at a bridal shop. When it came time to pick them up they were incomplete. The shop owner was behind schedule and she didn't let me know until the last minute. I was distraught. I called Mary to tell her what happened. She agreed to finish all the gowns herself. My sister-in-law was a lifesaver. She was so willing to do anything to make my day grand. She also had time to make mom's gown as well as her own.

Five months before the wedding day I became pregnant with Daniel's child. I wasn't happy about it. I already had Janel and I wasn't prepared for another.

One day Daniel and I went to play a game of pinochle with some friends of ours. They were heavy marijuana smokers. The four of us passed around one joint, a mixture of Columbian Gold and hashish. Eventually Angela and I left our men at the table playing the game. We moved to the bottom of the stairs and sat on the steps. We talked for several minutes. When we decided to return upstairs, neither one of us could get up. Our feet felt as if they were sealed in cement blocks. We looked at each other and laughed. Our only choice was to sit there a while longer. I told her about my pregnancy, that I had not yet informed Daniel.

"What are you going to do?" she asked.

"I don't know. I'm really not ready for another baby now. I believe it's too soon."

"I have an idea. I know of a concoction you can take. Wait here, I'll be right back."

Angela returned with a small bowl of applesauce and black pepper, lots of black pepper sprinkled on top.

"Here," she said. "Take this and eat all of it."

I tasted the stuff. It was too hot.

"I can't get this down. It's horrible," I cried.

"Okay, I have one more idea. Go get a bottle of mineral oil from the store. Drink the entire bottle at one time and the baby will slide out," she advised.

The very next day I went to purchase the mineral oil. I uncapped the bottle and turned it up to my mouth. It was so slimy and gross. As I downed the oil, I thought to myself. I have to do this. It slid down my throat with ease. I hated it but continued to drink until the bottle was empty. For several days I saw oily urine dripping in the toilet. At the end of the week I was still pregnant. I had to inform Daniel. He was somber at the news. The look on my face revealed that I wasn't pleased either.

"Well, what do you want to do?" he asked.

"I'm not ready for another child. It's too soon. I want an abortion. Besides, I won't be able to fit into my wedding gown. I refuse to walk down the aisle in church pregnant," I said.

"Okay, I will take care of it," he assured me.

He never flinched at the idea. I had an abortion five weeks into the pregnancy. The truth was, I wanted to test the waters of marriage before I was stuck with another child.

I planned for some of my closest friends to share in the big day but only one of them was available to be part of the wedding party. My friends weren't prepared to shell out the cost of the gowns, so I engaged my co-workers to be my bridesmaids.

In lieu of wedding gifts, I asked for turkey donations for the reception. Everything was going to plan until the wedding day. On February 22, 1975, I arrived at the church, excited and afraid at the same time. My attendants were there and my wedding coordinator was ready to assist me. She gathered everyone together, instructing them to perform as they did during the rehearsal the previous evening. Everyone took their positions. The music started to play. I stood in the vestibule, waiting. My coordinator walked over to me.

"It is time to begin," she said.

"No, we can't," I replied nervously. "The groom's family has not arrived."

"Okay, we will wait a few more minutes, then, we must proceed. We are already behind schedule."

Five minutes passed. Just as I was about to give the go-ahead to my coordinator, in they walked. The usher seated the groom's family, then, the music began again. The wedding party processed down the aisle. All eyes turned to the back of the church as the music continued to play. The ushers at the back struggled with the runner for the bride. They had a difficult time getting the creases out. After some time, the wedding march began. I processed down the aisle on the arm of my oldest brother. My father's legs were very weak and he didn't feel up to the challenge of doing the honors.

At the end of the ceremony, a reception was held on the lower level of the church. Everything was going fine until someone walked over to Daniel and informed him that water was leaking from his radiator. It wasn't long before Daniel, the best man and all the other male attendants had left the head table. My attendants and I were left sitting there while they laid on the ground in their rented tuxedos, trying to fix the car. The photographer didn't get any pictures of the head table except the bride and groom.

We had a second reception planned for just our family and closest friends at Daniel's parents' house. When we arrived, Daniel's youngest brother was overseeing the preparation there. Shortly after our guests assembled, I noticed that some of the bottles of alcoholic beverages had been opened. I dismissed it momentarily. I made my way around the room chatting with my guests when the cellar door opened. Approximately fifteen uninvited hoodlums marched out of the basement and headed for the front door without saying anything to anyone. They reeked of marijuana. Immediately I realized where the liquor went. I was livid. I turned to Daniel.

"How could your brother ruin, what should've been the happiest day of our lives?" Those hoodlums drank a lot of the liquor that was intended for our guests. Not only that, they had the audacity to come in this house and smoke 'pot' in the basement."

I was so distraught I wanted to cry. As the liquor ran out, our guests went home. What should have turned out to be a beautiful day was the beginning of a nightmare.

Daniel and I didn't have money to spend on the ideal honeymoon, so we stayed in town at a local hotel. I wasn't very happy about it, but I was willing to sacrifice my dream vacation for more important things.

He moved into my mother's house. We wanted to save for the purchase of a house so we agreed to spend the first year with her. We paid my mother rent which allowed us to accumulate the necessary funds.

Daniel indicated that he wanted to adopt Janel. He was very empathetic in regards to my previously embroiled relationship with Glen. Immediately upon the return from our honeymoon, he sought a lawyer and filed the paperwork. For the first time in my life, I felt safe and secure. I no longer worried about Glen impeding on my life.

Six months into the marriage, Daniel and I had our first argument. I don't remember what precipitated it but I remember a comment I made. Daniel was Catholic and I made a remark about him not ever exercising his Catholic faith. He didn't attend church and he didn't practice what he preached. It made Daniel furious and he flew into a rage. The next thing I knew, Daniel had knocked me down across the bed, pounding his fists into my back. My mother heard the ruckus and appeared in our bedroom doorway. Immediately, she tried to pull Daniel off of me.

"Take your hands off my daughter. If you ever touch her again you'll live to regret it," she yelled at him.

Several minutes later, after cooling off, Daniel apologized for his actions, but I saw Daniel in a different light. The young, quiet man I first met now exposed a hidden side to him.

A few weeks after the fight, my mother came to me to talk.

"Gerri, you should really try and talk to Rev. Williams. He counsels married couples, you know."

"I know, mom, but he just arrived at the church and I don't want to burden him right now with my problems."

"Well, you think about it. I believe he could be very helpful to you."

"Thanks mom. I will think about it."

Rev. Williams was the newly elected pastor to the church after the death of the former one. He was a minister of great vision and had started new programs and ministries at the church. Eventually I would contact him if necessary. I kept my mother's suggestion in mind.

The next six months were without incident. The possibility of Daniel becoming abusive again was at the back of my mind. If he hit you once, he'll hit you again, I thought.

Daniel and I decided we wanted to look for a home in Jersey so we went across the bridge. We didn't have to look very far. We found a brand new construction about five blocks from the bridge in Palmyra, NJ.

I resigned from my job in center city and decided I would look for work in the Jersey area. Before I left Philadelphia, Daniel drove me to the office so that I could say goodbye to all my friends. I walked around the office wishing everyone well and I must have been all of twenty minutes when Daniel appeared at the door. He was beckoning for me to come. I waved to all as I walked towards the exit. Daniel was standing on the other side of the door with a strange look in his eye. Before I could say anything he had snatched me by my collar and started dragging me down the stairs. I missed two and three steps at a time as I frantically tried to grab the handrail for support. Once I got to the bottom of the stairs I started yelling at him.

"What is wrong with you? Are you crazy?"

"What's wrong? Do you really want to know what's wrong? You took too long. I have things to do."

Daniel was screaming at me at the top of his lungs. I couldn't believe how fast he snapped over nothing. He threw open the car door and shoved me in. He got behind the wheel and continued screaming as he pulled away from the curb. A few minutes later, all of a sudden, the car stopped in the middle of the street. He looked down at the gas gauge. It rested on E.

"This is your fault," he yelled turning towards me.

Daniel slapped me so hard, I saw stars. My head throbbed.

"Get out of the car and walk to that gas station we just passed and get some gas," he ordered.

He thrust an empty, plastic container in my hand and forced me to go get gas while he stayed with the car. Tears streamed down my face and strands of hair covered my eyes as I walked to the gas station. My deepest fears were realized. I married a nut. He hid his private rage the entire time we dated. I hadn't a clue that he could be so abusive until our first fight. Daniel should have heeded my mother's words when she told him he would regret treating me this way. I had hoped that Daniel and I could make this marriage work, that my feelings for him would blossom into true love and respect, but I didn't see any chance of that happening now, not unless he sought professional help.

Shortly after leaving General Accident Assurance Co., I enrolled in a school for medical and dental assistants. For six months I learned the techniques of the medical field. I graduated at the top of my class. I did my one month internship at a doctor's office in Camden, NJ. I had great hands on experience with many aspects of the medical profession. I was now prepared to meet my new challenges as a medical assistant.

The school had a job placement program and they assigned students to work in different sections of the city and surrounding areas. The first day on the job in my new office, so many things went wrong. I walked into the reception area and the first thing I noticed was a huge cockroach crawling up the wall. Next, the doctor coughed up phlegm and spit in the trash can in one of the examining rooms. Then, a spaced-out drug addict walked in and went straight back to the examining room area without saying a word to anyone. I looked questionably at the other assistant in the office.

"Oh, don't worry about him. He does that all the time," she said.

I couldn't believe my ears or eyes. Before the day ended, law officers appeared in the doorway.

"Did anyone call the police?" one of them asked.

I stared in disbelief. I informed the doctor that I would not return.

"There is too much going on here. I'm done."

"Good," he replied. "I'll find someone else."

I called the school to report what had transpired. They told me, this particular doctor had a hard time keeping assistants. He constantly called the school for replacements.

"Don't worry. We will find you another office."

"That's okay, don't bother. I don't think I want to continue in this field," I replied.

I was disheartened with the whole thing. I walked away from the profession without looking back. I continued to search out God's plan for my life in the field of employment. Evidently, that wasn't it.

A few days later, Daniel and I had packed up all of our belongings for the move to New Jersey. I was anxious to see if living in our new home would make a difference in his attitude. For a while we were happy and getting along quite well. A month or two later, Daniel had regressed to his former temperament. Every little thing irritated him. It was becoming impossible to live with him. At times, it seemed, nothing made him happy.

"The house is dirty. Look at the floors. Dinner isn't ready. What have you been doing all day?"

I stood there, staring at him. I dared not say anything. He walked away and headed for the bedroom.

Two weeks later, Daniel entered the house. He just came home from work. He was upset when he realized that dinner hadn't been started.

"Why isn't dinner ready yet? You've been home all day, obviously, doing nothing."

Daniel flew into a rage. I picked up a pot and started filling it with hot water. While my back was turned he kicked me in the back of my thigh with the heavy boot he was wearing. My leg buckled beneath me and the water spilled out of the pot as I tried to regain my balance. I was fortunate that none of the hot water splashed on my hands. Immediately I applied ice to my thigh to reduce the pain and redness. A few days later, I noticed a huge horrible black and blue bruise, extending across the width of my thigh. It remained for a few weeks before my skin color returned to normal. I noticed that Daniel would hit me in places on my body that weren't visible to others. It was evident he didn't want people to know that he had been beating me.

In the weeks that followed, I concentrated on making an escape plan. I had no intention of remaining in a volatile relationship.

One day I walked into the recruitment center. I talked with the enlistment officer about joining the army. He asked me several questions and he gave me a competency test. I asked him questions as well.

"If I want to join the army, can anyone stop me?"

"No, but are you sure this is what you really want to do?"

He searched my eyes for the answer.

"Something tells me that you don't really want to join the army. You are married, aren't you? I believe that you are trying to get away from a bad marriage. If that is the case, you don't want to do this."

I thought about it for a while.

"You're right. I'll think of something else. Thanks for your time. You have been very helpful."

I rose to shake his hand and thanked him for his advice. I left the office with a different attitude, but with one that said, you can't run away from your problems.

My next plan was to store up small amounts of money, so I would have something to fall back on when I needed it. I found a place to hide money in the house. Eventually I would make my exit, I just didn't know when.

I started having bouts of depression. I stared aimlessly into space, hours at a time. I didn't feel like doing much of anything. My energy level was low and I often had crying spells.

Despite the rough patches, I really needed to concentrate on holding my marriage together. My main goal was to get Glen's grip loosened from Janel. He had no right, as far as I was concerned, to meddle in our lives. I just wanted to protect my daughter and give her a secure environment to grow up in. Both of us needed stability. I didn't know which was worse, Glen trying to prevent the adoption from behind bars or Daniel being so abusive.

In April, 1976, we received a letter from our lawyer stating that a hearing had been set up for us to meet with the judge in a room at the courthouse. He informed us that Glen would be brought to the proceedings because he was the biological father. The fact that I would come face to face with him once again unnerved me. I had hoped he wouldn't delay the adoption from taking place.

When it was time to appear for the court date, we arrived outside the courthouse. Our lawyer was inside waiting for us. He briefed us on what was going to take place. He told us to be prepared to answer questions from the judge. Once seated inside, Glen was brought in, handcuffed. They seated him across the table from us. He stared straight ahead, not making any eye contact with us. The judge asked Glen several questions, then Daniel. When it was over, he awarded custody to Daniel. It was only a matter of time before our lawyer would present the final papers to us. Glen appealed to the Supreme Court to have the judge's decision overturned, but it was denied. Thank God for big and small blessings.

Several months after we had settled into our house, Daniel came to me and told me he wanted a finished basement. He had contacted a contractor to give an estimate. When he had shared the details with me I told him I didn't think we should do it.

"Daniel, I'll need a car when I find a job. That's more important."

"Well, I'll talk to the contractor and tell him it's not feasible right now."

The next day Daniel had the contractor to come to the house. We sat around the table discussing the basement project.

"My wife wants a car, so the basement might have to wait."

What if I told you that you could have both," the contractor said.

"How can we do that?" asked Daniel.

"I can bring the estimate for the basement in at a higher amount. When you go to the bank for the loan, I will go with you. I will do the basement for the amount I originally quoted. You can purchase the car with the overage. Would that make you both happy?"

"How you swing it is up to you. All I'm saying is, I need a car."

A few days later, Daniel and the contractor went to the bank to secure the loan. Once the work began on the house, the contractor went to the car dealer with us to purchase my new car. We roamed around the lot searching for the perfect car for me. Daniel found a cute little Plymouth, Arrow. I fell in love with it. I opened the door to look inside.

"It's nice but it's a stick shift." I don't know how to drive it."

"Daniel, are you going to teach me how to drive this car?" I asked.

"No, I'm not going to teach you. I don't give driving lessons."

"If you decide to get this car, I'll teach you how to drive it," the contractor said.

We decided to get the car. The contractor drove the car back to our house and parked it on the driveway. Daniel and I pulled in behind him. The car remained parked for the next three weeks.

One day the contractor left his crew working on the basement while he took me out for driving lessons. We went to an empty supermarket lot where he gave me lessons. It took me a while to get the hang of it. By the third day, I was becoming used to the stick shift. I liked it very much, even better than the automatic. I could drive the car on level ground but I had trouble on hills.

The next day I went over to Philly to get my girlfriend, Margie. I took her for a ride in my new car. I was doing fine until I came to an intersection with an incline. I had trouble equalizing from the accelerator to the clutch. We missed three green lights. The car cut off several times. The people behind me were getting irate. Margie and I were laughing hysterically. The guy behind me wanted to move my car out of the way for me. Finally, I managed to get the car to engage and off we went. I didn't have any more problems on hills after that. I became a pro and the stick shift became my friend.

Each day I searched the newspaper want ads. It wasn't long before I found a keypunch position. That was good. I was a skilled keypuncher and that job would be perfect for me. I called for an interview and I was hired within a week. There were two shifts available, day and night. I chose the night shift. The hours were from midnight to eight o'clock in the morning. Daniel worked days. We became like two ships passing in the night. I avoided sleeping next to Daniel which made me very happy.

For a time, everything was peaceful in the house. The midnight shift kept a rift from occurring most of the time. Daniel's temperament was still something to be reckoned with. One day an argument broke out between Daniel and I while in our bedroom. He was screaming at the top of his lungs, like usual. We bickered back and forth for several minutes.

"I am so glad I don't have any more children right now. This is not the environment to raise a healthy family in," I added.

"The only reason I paid for that abortion is because I never believed that baby was mine," he screamed at me.

His fists went flying into my head and chest. Daniel left the bedroom. After every fight he would walk away. I sat on the edge of the bed crying, unaware that Janel was standing in the doorway, watching. She walked up to me and patted me on my shoulder.

"Are you okay, mommy? I love you," she said.

I wrapped my arms around my little girl and said,

"I love you too, baby. We're both going to be okay," I promised her. I left the room to find Daniel.

"Don't you ever expose Janel to your violent rage again," I warned.

Then I stormed out of the kitchen.

In the coming days, the peaceful evenings in the house were a blessing. One weekend I was very tired and I decided to go to bed earlier than usual. Daniel was up and about. Later that evening I heard Daniel when he climbed into bed beside me. In the early morning hours after midnight I started to dream. It was a very frightening thing. The mattress on our bed took on the form of a very heavy chunk of metal. I was running around trying to get away from it because it was trying to crush me. I started screaming. Daniel grabbed me, trying desperately to awaken me. Instead of waking me up, I snatched him into the dream with me. Now the metal chunk was trying to crush both of us.

"Gerri, wake up, wake up," he hollered.

When I finally opened my eyes, I realized I was on the opposite side of the bed. Daniel's hands were around my waist. He had tackled me to the floor.

"What happened?" I asked.

"You were having a nightmare," he said.

"Daniel, when you grabbed me, instead of waking me up, I snatched you into the nightmare with me. How could that be?" I asked, puzzled.

"I don't know, Gerri. All I know is that you were running around the room screaming."

I climbed back in the bed with my eyes wide open until I was able to relax and go back to sleep. When daybreak came I relived the scene of the nightmare. Throughout the day I was bothered by the experience. I couldn't stop thinking about it. I came to the conclusion that it was possibly stress which triggered it. I've never had a nightmare before and I hoped I'd never have another.

A week had passed since that horrible nightmare. I tried to relax more but the constant bickering between Daniel and I increased as the weeks went on. It wasn't easy trying to find common ground where Daniel would be receptive to compromise. It just didn't seem to exist.

I entered the house. The silence consumed my thoughts and I wondered what I could do for my husband to please him today, just to see a smile on his face, one that would let me know that he was in a good mood. I wanted to be the wife who ran to the door when I heard the key turn in the lock, greeting my husband with a warm hug and kiss, one that says I am glad that you are home. Deep in my heart I longed for that type of relationship.

Today I decided that I would vacuum the carpets, since that's what my husband complained about the most–dirt.

He would examine the carpets for specks of lint particles or debris deposited by peoples' shoes.

My mind wandered aimlessly as I recalled the arguments and fights we have had, over anything and everything. My eyes filled with water and I felt a tear slowly trickle down one cheek as I stood in the center of the floor of my smallest bedroom.

I turned my focus to my Lord and Savior and began to pray.

"Lord, I am so tired of going through this mess. Please give my husband an understanding heart. Why can't I get this right? Please watch over me as I try to make this marriage work. I need you Lord now more than ever. Please protect me from this abuse I am suffering."

As I fought back the tears which now streamed freely down my face, I walked to the closet and slid back the door. I reached for the vacuum cleaner and pulled it out. Glancing around the room, my eyes searched for a wall outlet. Through the tears that now blinded me, I groped for the end of the plug and pushed it in. I tapped the switch on the cleaner and pushed the vacuum back and forth. My mind drifted back to my husband. I thought to myself, he will be happy to see the carpets clean when he gets home. Maybe he will be in a good mood when he walks in. I continued for several minutes pulling back and forth on the handle when I heard someone call out to me.

"Gerri," the voice called.

Startled, I shut my vacuum cleaner off and stood there listening for what seemed like an eternity. The house was deathly silent.

"Hmmm," I said.

It must be my imagination, I thought. I waited a few more seconds then decided to resume my cleaning. I turned the vacuum cleaner back on and continued the strokes back and forth.

"Gerri," the voice called again.

I stood petrified for a few seconds recalling what my mother once told me. She said, if someone calls your name and you don't know who it is, don't answer. I shut the cleaner off again and decided I was going to walk around the house. I went from room to room and didn't see nor hear anyone. My imagination started to play tricks on me. Had someone entered the house? I didn't know. I called out my husband's name, thinking he might have come home early and had gone to the basement…nothing, no noise, no human voices. I proceeded to the basement door and asked myself should I open it? Slowly I turned the knob and pulled the door towards me. It was dark down there. No one could descend those steps without making noise. I hesitated for a few minutes, peering down at the darkness. I thought it best not to turn the light on, nor descend the stairs. I closed the door and headed towards the living room. I went to the front door and flung it open. I stepped out onto the porch and walked to one end and peered around the side of the house. There was no one in sight. I turned to walk to the opposite end of the porch and looked around the other side, still no one. It was too quiet, not a bird chirped, not a dog barked. There were no children playing outside, just the stillness of the day. You could hear a pin drop. I stood lost in thought for several seconds. Finally, I reentered the house, heading for the bedroom where I was cleaning.

I stood in the bedroom doorway, reflecting on what I had heard several minutes earlier. The voice was real. It was very distinct. I could hear every syllable and consonant in my name. No one has ever pronounced my name so clearly.

Then I realized where the voice had come from. It had to be a divine presence. I dropped to the floor and the tears once again started to stream down my face. With my knees drawn to my chest I lowered my head, resting my forehead between my knees. I cried out.

"Thank you, Lord, for listening to me."

Several minutes passed as I sat there and meditated. An inner peace swept over me. The tears dried on my face. Finally, I rose to my feet to inspect the carpet. It looked very clean. I walked to the bathroom and reached for my wash cloth. I turned the spigot on, placing my hands under the warm, running water. I held the cloth over my eyes. Looking in the mirror I could see they were quite red and puffy. After hanging the cloth on the rack I flicked off the switch and returned to the bedroom. I pulled the plug, wound the coil around the holder and pushed the cleaner back into the closet. As I slid the door shut, I heard someone at the front door. I walked to the hallway and waited for the door to open. I waited to see if my husband would be in a good mood or not. I heard the key turn in the lock. The door swung open and Daniel walked in. He entered with a smile on his face. I smiled back at him, happy to see him in a good mood for a change.

"So what have you been doing today?" he asked.

"I have been vacuuming the carpets and now I am going to get dinner started."

I said nothing of the revelation which occurred several minutes earlier.

CHAPTER 6

August, 1977, I heard that Western Union Telegraph Co. was starting a new training class. They had open positions for new operators. It sounded very interesting and I wanted to enroll in the class. The training started from 3:00 p.m. to 11:30 p.m. for one month. I decided to apply. I was tired of keypunching and I wanted to advance my skills.

I had to be at work at midnight. I didn't know how I could do both. It was very challenging. When I got home in the morning, I went right to sleep. Daniel had to do most of the cooking. By the third week I could hardly function. I asked my boss for a week off. I told her I was involved in a program at the University of Penn for a study of people suffering from depression. I was given the time off.

There were three weeks of classroom training and one week of on-the-floor training. It was crucial that I pass or I would be terminated. I gave it my all. At the end of the week, I was notified I had succeeded in graduating to the floor. I was hired.

I returned to my job to pick up my last check. Instead of working that night, I decided I would go to sleep in the lounge. My supervisor came to the lounge two or three times to wake me up. I pretended not to hear her. When it was time to go home, I got up and left the lounge. On my way down the hall leading to the outside door, I passed my supervisor. She was, no doubt, headed to the lounge to get me. When I came face to face with her I said, you don't have to worry about firing me because I quit. I left there happy, knowing I had a new job awaiting me.

Shortly after landing the Western Union job, the testing for the postal service opened. Daniel always encouraged me to enter the postal service, because he was a mailman. Many times he would say to me, take the test.

"The job has a lot of benefits and the salary is good too. It takes a while to get in because you go to a list determined by your test score. In most cases it could take up to a year or more to get hired."

"Okay," I'll take the test and see what happens."

When the test opened weeks later, I was there. It was an easy test and I though I did well. From that day forward, it was a wait and see process.

In the weeks that followed, signs of Daniel's rage resurfaced. The least little thing would set him off. One day in the middle of an argument, I told him how ridiculous he was for getting angry at little, petty things that just didn't make sense.

At times he would holler at Janel for not picking up her toys. He walked barefooted often, and stepped on sharp objects.

"Daniel, don't yell at her like that. She's a child. Talk to her in a softer tone. You are frightening her and I don't like it."

"She has to learn how to cooperate with me and do as she's told."

"You can't win the heart of a child when you act the way you do."

My new job kept me thoroughly engaged. I learned how to send candy grams, money orders, mailgrams, typewritten and singing telegrams and so forth. I was graded on proficiency at unawares and excelled in my typing skills. I felt good about going to work. I enjoyed talking to people in all walks of life. I had the opportunity to talk to famous movie stars. At a time in my life when my marriage was so rocky, my job compensated temporarily for my unhappiness. The singing telegrams were the most hilarious. I would call a customer with the singing telegram and say, "Can I read your telegram or do I have to sing it?"

"Sing it, of course," would be the reply.

I cleared my throat and gave it my best shot. The customer and I roared with laughter. Despite the doom and gloom at home, I managed to have a few bright days in my life when I forgot about my troubles for a fleeting moment.

The next altercation between Daniel and I resulted in me seeking medical attention. He punched me in the top of my head so viciously that a soft spot or bubble formed. I told Daniel I was going to the hospital and I took his health insurance card with me.

"Your health plan is going to pay for this check-up," I said.

Early the next morning I headed for the hospital to have my head injury checked. The doctor didn't find anything serious to worry about. That was comforting to hear. I told him about having severe migraine headaches. He gave me a prescription for Cafergot. I didn't know if my headaches were contributed to the beatings or something else. I took the medication as prescribed.

The following day I was back at work. I was on the phone line with a customer, typing a very long mailgram when I noticed that some of the words were scrambled. Once I released the customer from the call, it was customary for me to proofread my work before transmission. Several words were misspelled. All the letters in the word were correct but in the wrong order. I corrected the document and took my next call. It happened again and again. I unplugged my headset. I paused for several seconds as my eyes filled with tears. I felt so inadequate. I focused my attention on the front of the room where my supervisor was eyeing me intently. Why did I think I could function as usual? Once I composed myself, I plugged my headset back in to wait for the next call. When the call came through, I heard a click in my line, indicating that my supervisor was listening in on the call. I continued to work as usual, asking the customer the necessary questions to complete his telegram. When I had finished, I disconnected the caller. While checking the message for accuracy, my supervisor interrupted me.

"Unplug your headset," Tim said.

I looked up to see Tim headed down the aisle. He stopped at my desk.

"Gerri, let's go for a walk."

I placed my headset on the desk and allowed Tim to lead me out of the room. We walked around the circumference of the building.

"What's wrong? It's clear that something's bothering you."

I looked up at Tim.

"I'm fine. I just needed a little break," I lied.

"You're not fine. You are a basket case. You are being abused at home, aren't you?" he asked.

"How did you know?"

"I have my way of knowing these things. Are you afraid to go home?"

"No, I'll be all right."

"If you need to talk, let me know. Here is my phone number."

Tim reached for a pen and scribbled his number on a piece of paper and handed it to me.

"Thanks for your concern, Tim."

Tim was known for lending a sympathetic ear when his workers had problems and people found it easy to talk to him. He never pushed but offered his assistance wherever he could. I folded the paper and shoved it in my pocket. Tim led me back to my seat. I plugged in my headset and waited for the next call. He returned to his station at the head of the room. The walk cleared my head.

When my shift ended I hurried to my car. I got in but I didn't start the engine right away. I sat lost in thought for several minutes. It hit me all of a sudden. I was tired of going home to the same old crap. I didn't want to face Daniel. The tears started to fall. As I sat behind the wheel waiting for my vision to clear I thought about where I wanted to go. I wiped my eyes with the back of my sleeve and started the engine.

I decided that I was going to find my pastor up at the university where he taught. The drive was about two hours away. I pointed my car in the direction of the Poconos. Three hours later I hadn't arrived at my destination. I ended up practically from where I started. I was very upset by now but I didn't give up. I gassed up my car for the long journey. I was so tired but I knew I had to find my way this time. I got directions from the attendant and took off. Total time spent on the road was five hours. When I arrived, it was almost 10:00 p.m. I approached the door to Rev. Williams' class. He was sitting on the edge of his desk, lecturing. I opened the door slightly to get his attention. When he glanced up and saw me, I gently closed it. He came to the door and invited me in. I took an empty seat and waited for the class to end. Once the students vacated the room, I remained. I related what happened.

Rev. Williams registered me in a hotel room then he called Daniel.

"Gerri is here with me. She came to the university. She is very upset right now. I will bring her home tomorrow."

After hanging up, Rev. Williams turned to me.

"Try to get some rest tonight. I will call you in the morning."

"Okay, thank you for your help," I replied.

Rev. Williams left the room. I crawled into bed and cried myself to sleep.

In the morning he returned to the hotel to pick me up and he followed me back to my house. When we arrived, Daniel seemed to be in a good mood. Rev. Williams talked with him a while. When he felt it was safe to leave me there and I, likewise, he left. Daniel remained in a good mood for the next several days.

I discussed with Daniel about seeking advice on our marriage and how we could go about making the necessary adjustments for better communication between us. He agreed to talk with my pastor. It wasn't long before I was on the phone talking with Rev. Williams about setting up a counseling appointment. He agreed to come to our house and talk to both of us. The appointment was set up for a Monday morning.

Sunday came and I prepared to go to church. My attendance had fallen off drastically since moving to Jersey but I managed to send my offering to the church or I would take it whenever I could. This particular Sunday Daniel asked me to stay home and go with him to the park for a picnic.

"Daniel, you know my church life comes first. I have missed many Sundays already and I want to go today. There is a special service this afternoon and I want to be there. You have been managing to keep me away many times but not today, Daniel. I am going to the service. You can do what you want," I said.

I hurried to my car and got in. I backed out of the driveway and pointed my car in the direction of Philadelphia. When I arrived at church, I felt better. I was surrounded by my friends. My moments of unhappiness disappeared.

I didn't have Janel to worry about. She happened to be at my mother's house. She often stayed with her grandmother during the summer months. I didn't want her subjected to Daniel's constant rants.

I enjoyed the church service very much but as I sat there I thought about Daniel's pleas to keep me home because he wanted to go to the park. It plagued my mind so much, that I decided to forgo the afternoon service. Instead, I would go home and surprise Daniel and go to the park, just as he wanted. When I rounded the corner to my house I was the one who got the surprise. On my driveway was his friend's car. He and his wife were washing their car. I pulled in front of the house and parked. In a chair on the porch sat the woman's sister. I spoke to all of them as I passed by. I opened the door and entered the house. Daniel was in the kitchen, standing at the sink, rinsing a small turkey. He set it on the countertop and turned to look at me as I entered.

"I thought you were going to be at church all day. I'm glad you're here. You can cook this meat while I'm gone. We're going to the park."

"Your meat will be waiting for you when you get back. I'm not cooking anything."

"Suit yourself. I'll see you later."

Daniel hurried out the door and five minutes later, they were gone.

I stood there in shock. I couldn't believe I had given up my church program for this.

I looked at the turkey sitting there on the countertop. I opened the refrigerator door and shoved it in.

The more I thought about it, the more convinced I was that God put me in this place, at this time for a reason. I had no problem putting two and two together. Daniel was having an affair. My eyes were finally open.

Well, if he thinks I'm staying home, cooking while he's gallivanting around with another woman, he's got another thought coming.

At nine o'clock the next morning, Rev. Williams arrived for our counseling session. I was in the process of fixing breakfast. I fixed something for the two of us and sat down to eat.

"Where is Daniel?" he asked.

"I don't know. He didn't come home last night," I replied. "He knew about the appointment this morning; so much for trying to save our marriage. This is the perfect example of why there is no hope for us; not only is he violent, but now he's cheating."

"How do you know he's cheating?"

"He left here yesterday with a woman and he hasn't returned yet. Rev. Williams, I really don't know what you could say at this point that is going to change this situation."

As we ate quietly, I heard Daniel open the door. Daniel greeted Rev. Williams as he entered the kitchen.

"Did you fix breakfast for me too, Gerri?"

I looked him up and down. He had a spot on his T-shirt and it wasn't dirt.

"Why didn't you eat where you slept last night?"

I didn't want to take any food away from the woman and her child."

"Well, you should've thought about that when you left yesterday."

Daniel walked over to the stove and started preparing his own breakfast.

Rev. Williams sat there speechless for several minutes, watching our interaction with one another. When Daniel had finished his breakfast, we sat down to talk. In the back of my mind it meant absolutely nothing. I was angry. I was more determined than ever to find a way out.

In the weeks that followed, I continued to seek advice from Rev. Williams during the times when I felt it necessary. He was a great source of help to me. I knew deep down I would have to make some serious decisions regarding my marriage.

Rev. Williams wasn't so quick to give up. He was in the process of forming a young married couples group at the church. He encouraged us to participate. The group would meet once each month at a different house, hosted by one of the married couples. The discussion would consist of different topics. The main goal was to discover how to resolve conflict and open up new avenues of communication. It was also geared to maintaining a healthy marital relationship. At the conclusion of the meeting, dinner, hors d'oeuvres, or refreshments were served. Daniel and I hosted one of the meetings. The group lasted for several months but eventually, the married couples bowed out of their commitment to participate. Ultimately, the group disbanded.

As the arguing and fighting continued in our home, I became despondent at times. I spent less and less time with my friends and less time at church. Whenever I spent time in Philadelphia, Daniel would complain and ask where I had been. One day he let it slip that he knew exactly how many miles I had driven. At that point I realized he was recording the mileage whenever he became suspicious of my whereabouts.

I began to drink beer and wine more frequently, but not to the point of intoxication. I soothed my nerves with small amounts of alcohol. I recalled the time when my mother worried about my alcohol intake. She was afraid that I was following in the footsteps of my father. Thank God I still had some self-control over my life. With all my crutches in place—beer, wine and cigarettes—I managed to get through each day. Eventually things took its toll on me.

Days later, I sat at my kitchen table. I was alone. Many thoughts ran through my mind. I began to cry as I remembered all the horrible disagreements Daniel and I have had. More and more I started to feel isolated. I was becoming detached from myself. I felt as if I were two people instead of one. My head ached. I continued to suffer from migraine headaches. I picked up my bottle of Cafergot pills and stared at the bottle. I filled a glass with water and sat it in front of me. I opened the pill bottle and removed two pills. I swallowed them. I sat at the table for a long time. I waited to see if my head would stop pounding. Depression set in. I was staring into space for several minutes. Bad thoughts crept through my pounding head. I picked up the bottle of Cafergot and started swallowing pills one by one. It must have been twelve or fourteen pills I had taken. I sat there, completely lost in thought, feeling sorry for myself. I looked down into the bottle of pills and realized they were almost gone. I started crying. I needed attention. I didn't want to die. Not really. I had no idea what this medication might do to me. I picked up the phone and dialed 911.

"What's your emergency?" the voice at the other end asked.

"I need an ambulance. I just swallowed several pills."

Less than five minutes, the paramedics arrived. I opened the door to let them in.

"What did you take?" one of them inquired.

I showed them the bottle.

"Cafergot," I replied.

"How many did you take?"

"I don't know," I replied.

The attendants strapped me on the gurney and carried me out. When I arrived at the hospital, they pumped my stomach. Afterwards they asked several questions. The nurse had a form in her hand and she was writing my responses down.

"You took an overdose of medication. Why?'

"I wasn't trying to kill myself. If I wanted to do that I wouldn't have called the ambulance. I'm crying out for help. Can't you understand that?"

When they were ready to release me, they called Daniel and related what transpired. He came to the hospital to pick me up. The ride home was very quiet. He acted as if nothing was seriously wrong. He helped me get into bed. I flipped my tear stained pillow over a few times before I fell asleep.

The next two days I didn't feel like going to work, so I called out. I needed to take a little time to recover from my ordeal. I didn't want to be around anyone, not even Daniel.

He was quiet for the most part. I guess he didn't know what to say, so he said very little.

When I returned to work, I tried to gain a sense of normalcy. My inner spirit was in shambles but I kept it hidden. I surrounded myself with people who could make me laugh so that I would soon forget what had happened. I was so glad Janel was in Philadelphia with my mother and not a witness to any of this mess. When I look back on how nice the relationship was nine months before the marriage, I couldn't imagine my life ever amounting to this.

CHAPTER 7

It was mid-spring, 1978. I bumped into Jill. She was a childhood friend of mine. We grew up on the same street. As life went on we slowly drifted away. I moved away from the neighborhood at age eleven. The last time I saw Jill was on her wedding day when she married Johnny, the love of her life. I heard they had moved to Florida in 1974. It was two and a half years later when she returned to her hometown.

"Hi Jill, how are you? I haven't seen you in a long time."

"Johnny, I and our two kids have been living in Florida and now we are back."

"It's good to see you again. We have to catch up. It's been a while."

"Yes, it has. So, what's up with you?"

"I got married in 1975 and I'm living in Jersey now. I married one of Dee-Dee's neighbors. His name is Daniel. I am living in an abusive relationship though. Every day that goes by, I pray for things to change for the better."

"Oh, I'm sorry to hear that."

"Well, the truth is, you don't really know a person until you live with them."

"That's true."

From that day on, Jill and I kept in contact with each other.

Several days later, the phone rang. I picked it up.

"Hello," I said.

Jill was on the other end of the line. She proceeded to tell me that she and Johnny were looking for a place to stay. She said their landlord weren't fixing things up and they didn't have hot water. Daniel sat across from me as I talked. I related to him what Jill was saying. Daniel got on the phone and talked with Johnny and Jill. I heard him invite them to come live with us for a while. Within a few days, Jill and her family moved into our house with us. I was ecstatic. I thought to myself. Surely Daniel wouldn't raise his hand at me in front of them. I began to feel a new sense of security, protected by the presence of my friends.

After a few weeks, Daniel started showing his true colors. He was making rules for the household.

"No smoking in the house. I'm allergic to smoke," Daniel said to Johnny.

Johnny complied. We both stood on the porch whenever we wanted a cigarette.

One day, Jill told me that Daniel taped a picture of a black lung to the kitchen wall.

"Gerri, did you see the picture your husband taped to the wall?" Jill asked.

"No, I didn't," I replied.

Jill pointed to the picture that Daniel hung up.

I turned to look at it. "I guess that's to discourage us from smoking, no doubt," I replied.

A week or two later, Daniel was walking around shouting, lights out by nine o'clock.

In the privacy of our bedroom, I confronted Daniel.

"You can't tell people when to turn the lights out. This is not a prison. They are paying rent."

"This is my house. I can say whatever I want," he shouted.

"Okay, we'll see how far that rule goes," I said.

As time went on, Johnny and Jill were getting very annoyed with Daniel's mood swings. They were searching for a home in the Jersey area. They soon found a house around the corner from us.

"We hope to be approved for a mortgage to purchase the house we found," Jill said.

"Oh great, then you will be nearby," I replied.

I walked around the corner to look at the house they were interested in. It was very nice, lots of yard in the front and back. In the meantime, they continued to put up with the frustrations of Daniel.

We blended the two families as much as possible. We would alternate on a cooking schedule. Some days Jill would prepare the dinner for everybody and other times I would cook the meals. One day, Jill and I were talking about cooking. Jill offered to make a special dish for dinner.

"Let's not tell our husbands. It can be a surprise," I suggested.

"Okay," Jill agreed.

We began looking in the cabinets and refrigerator for the ingredients to make the meal. While searching, we were laughing and talking as girlfriends do. Daniel came home and asked what we were doing. I told him that we were fixing a surprise meal. He began asking over and over again.

"What are you making? What are you making?"

We continued laughing and jokingly said, "If we told you, it wouldn't be a surprise."

Without warning, Daniel stepped to me and punched me in the head. I fell to the floor and he started yelling at me.

"Don't f—with my head. When I ask you a question, I want an answer."

Jill looked on, flabbergasted. She couldn't believe what she had just witnessed. After he hit me, he looked at Jill.

"Well Jill, I guess now you see how I am. I just want you to know that I can handle even some of the biggest men."

That really angered Jill. She took it as a threat against her husband.

"Do you mean Johnny?" she asked.

He answered back quickly.

"No, no, that's not what I meant at all. I was just making a statement."

When Johnny got home, Jill told him what happened. Daniel never approached him.

A few weeks later, I was working in the delivery department. I had a lot of idle time between calls. Once in a while I would call my husband to say hello and check on things at home. This particular evening I had made several calls to the house but I didn't get an answer. I knew Daniel was home, I just couldn't understand why he wasn't answering the phone. I became a little anxious and I knew I had to work until midnight. When I arrived home, all of the lights were on and a U-Haul truck was parked in front of the door. Immediately, I knew something was seriously wrong. I parked my car on the driveway behind Daniel's and entered the house. I walked to my bedroom. Daniel was standing over by the wall with a wild, evil look in his eyes.

"Daniel, what happened here tonight?" I asked.

"I want these crazy people out of my house right now. They're not welcome here anymore."

I found Johnny and Jill packing. I asked Jill what had happened. She told me that she and Johnny had to go on an errand. They asked Daniel if they could leave their two girls at the house with him and Janel until they got back. He said yes. When they returned, their oldest daughter, who was six, came to her with a strange look on her face. Jill asked her if she was all right. She began to cry and said it was Mr. Daniel. I asked her, what about Mr. Daniel, but she cried harder. I called Johnny and told him to go talk to Daniel and find out what he said or did to her to make her so upset.

Johnny confronted Daniel in his bedroom to ask what happened. Daniel became very angry and started yelling at Johnny saying he doesn't have to take this mess from anyone and we need to get out of his house. The more Johnny asked, the more Daniel yelled "get out now." At that point, I went to his room to see what was going on. Johnny was fed up with Daniel's screaming and slapped him. Daniel went flying across the bed. As he got up, he was repeating, he needed medical attention. He then went for the phone. I didn't know who he was calling. We soon found out that it was the police. That's when Johnny began slapping him over and over again. I called out to Johnny to stop when I realized that Daniel was the type that would beat a woman, but not raise his hand to another man.

When the police arrived, Daniel told them that Johnny had hit him. We explained that he did or said something to our six year old. The police tried to talk to her and she just cried and cried. They told Daniel that he could press charges on Johnny for hitting him. They told us that we also had the right to press charges against Daniel because it appeared he did something to our daughter, which was why she was so upset. Instantly, Daniel changed his mind about pressing charges. Later when I talked to my daughter, she said he yelled at her.

"Where are you going to go this time of night?" I asked.

"We're going to Johnny's mother's house until we make settlement."

"Okay, I'm sorry it came to this. Now you know what I've been dealing with day in and day out."

After all of their belongings were loaded on the truck, Johnny turned to me and said.

"Gerri, when you are ready to leave that crazy husband of yours, you're welcome to come live with us."

"Thank you, I appreciate your offer. The way things are going around here, I'll probably be right behind you."

I watched Johnny, Jill and their two children pull away from the house. I felt safe for tonight. I didn't believe that Daniel had any energy left to start with me. I wondered how long it would be before the fighting would return. After a few more hours of listening to Daniel rant about what took place, I finally dozed off.

Two weeks after Johnny and Jill left, they made settlement on the house around the corner from us. I was very happy to know that they were close by. I went to visit them and kept them up to date on things.

As time went on, I had less and less to say to Daniel. He continued to order me around. Do this and do that. I was sick of the attitude. His mood swings were up and down. One afternoon Daniel wanted intimacy. I just wasn't in the mood. He became very agitated and started hollering. Next thing I knew, his fists were flying again. Daniel threw me down on the bed and forced himself on me.

"You are my wife. When I want sex, you're supposed to comply," he yelled.

"Oh really, you beat me like a drum and I'm supposed to be intimate with you? Are you really that crazy, Daniel?"

"Get up and fix me a sandwich. I'm hungry, he snapped. "There's tuna fish in the refrigerator."

Daniel shoved me out of the bedroom.

"Fix me a sandwich now!" he ordered.

I was angry as hell. I walked to the kitchen, battered and humiliated. I can't take this anymore, I thought to myself. My mind started wandering and I conjured up evil thoughts, ways to get even with Daniel. I was very tired of the abuse. It was so overwhelming. I started to make his sandwich. I gave back to Daniel what he had given me. I spread the mayonnaise on the bread. I slapped the tuna on top of the bread and placed the sandwich on a saucer. Then I called him to the table.

"Your sandwich is ready."

Daniel sat down at the table to prepare to eat. He picked up his sandwich and bit into it.

"Do you want some?" he offered.

He was acting as if nothing happened. I felt so much contempt but I didn't show it.

"No thank you," I responded with a devilish grin.

I watched him eat until the sandwich was gone. I left Daniel sitting there and walked away.

One day I went to my secret hiding place. I counted the money I had saved up. It was about a thousand dollars. I was pleased. I carefully returned the money to its hidden spot. A smile came over my face as I contemplated my next move.

The arguments continued on a weekly basis, mostly minor in nature. The tension remained high. I tried everything in my power to avoid a confrontation with him.

I was sitting in my living room resting. It was the middle of the afternoon. Daniel sat in the chair next to me. He got up and went to one of the bedroom closets and came back with a red leather jacket. He handed me the jacket and said he wanted his missing button sewn on.

I took the jacket and threaded the needle. It was very hard to sew.

"Daniel, I can't sew this button on. I don't have the right size needle. This is leather."

"Well, do the best you can. I'll look for one."

He got up to search. He returned with a larger needle.

"Here, try this, he said."

Daniel eyed me intently as I sewed the button on. All of a sudden Daniel jumped up out of the chair and snatched the jacket from my hands. He put the coat on and glanced down at it.

"You've sewn it on crooked," he shouted at me. "Take it out and do it over," he demanded.

I became frustrated. Daniel sat back down in the chair, his eyes cutting daggers at me. A few minutes later, Daniel shouted.

"Give me the jacket. You can't do a damn thing right."

I held the jacket out to Daniel with the tip of my middle finger. He reached for the jacket. When I thought he had grasped it, I let it go. The jacket fell between the two chairs. He jumped up screaming that I had thrown his jacket on the floor. Daniel punched me in my arms and chest. At the end of the altercation, resentment started to build up. I walked to the front door and flung it open. I needed to cool down so I breathed in some fresh air.

It was nearing September. Daniel's moods were unpredictable, his moves, calculating. I avoided as many incidents as possible. Once in a while he made reference to the time that Johnny and Jill were with us and how glad he was that they were gone.

"You know, Gerri, if you're not happy here, you can leave too," he retorted.

You just don't know. I plan to do just that, I thought to myself.

Day after day, I continued to live in this abusive relationship, not knowing how much more I could endure. At some point in time, I would have to conclude that enough is enough. It was the next fight that would bring me to the realization that my marriage was over.

I don't even remember what precipitated the final fight. I had been hit in the head several times throughout the marriage and so many arguments over dumb, senseless things, it no longer mattered why, or what. I remember Daniel shouting at the top of his lungs. I was arguing back at him. Daniel emerged from the bedroom and started coming towards me. I was standing in the living room. He walked up to me with both fists aimed at me. Daniel sucker punched me as his right fist went into my chest and the left one in my back simultaneously. I dropped to the floor like a ton of bricks. He walked away from me. I tried to get up but couldn't. I laid there, gasping for air. I couldn't breathe normally so I had to catch my breath through my mouth. I dragged myself across the floor. It was imperative that I get out the front door before he returned. As I crawled out the door, I saw my neighbors' door open across the street. I knew they could hear what was going on over here. Daniel was so loud when he argued. By the time I reached the end of the driveway, I tried to stand up but I couldn't. Bent over and breathing through my mouth, I slowly made my way to their door in a stooped position. Lionel was standing there.

He opened the screen door to let me in. His wife, Lydia, was behind him. They told me they heard the commotion.

"Are you going to call the police?" they asked.

"Yes, I have to. I need to get my belongings from the house."

Lionel called the police for me. I remained at their house until they arrived. By that time, I was able to stand with some discomfort. I related to the officers what took place.

"Do you want to press charges against your husband, ma'am?"

"What does that mean for me?" I asked.

"Well, unless we actually see him hit you, we can't hold him for long. He will be released in the morning."

"In other words, you're telling me that I may not be safe once you release him?"

The officer nodded.

"Forget it, I'm not pressing charges. I just want my things out of the house."

"We will accompany you to the house and wait while you get what you need."

I entered the house with the officers close behind. Daniel was in the bedroom standing by the wall, near the window. He stared at us as I entered to remove some clothes and my secret stash of money I had hidden. One police officer stood guard in the bedroom doorway. The other stood in the corridor. I told them I would come back for the rest of my things at a later date. They advised me to come to the police station for an escort first before re-entering the premises. When I had gathered all that I needed, I headed for the front door. Daniel called out to me.

"Wait a minute, Gerri. You are not leaving here with the car. It is mine."

"No Daniel, it isn't. I'm taking the car."

"I bought the car."

"You bought it in my name, your mistake."

One of the officers asked Daniel for the title. When he produced it, he handed it to the officer. The officer looked at Daniel.

"The car belongs to her."

He handed the title to me.

"Thank you," I said to the officer with a big smile on my face.

I left the house. I got into my Plymouth Arrow and took off, headed to my mother's house. As I drove, the pain in my chest eased somewhat and my breathing returned to normal. Daniel had hit me so hard I thought my lungs had collapsed. It turned out, that he had just knocked the wind out of me. I was glad to be out of there. Finally I was on the road to freedom.

I had so much on my mind. Over and over, my marriage played in my head. It was more bad than good. I never anticipated that I would be living in such a nightmare as this. I was blessed, in that, I had escaped serious injury. Daniel never pulled a knife, gun or anything else on me. His fists were his only weapon.

When I look back from the beginning of my relationship with Daniel, all I could think about is how I could flee from Glen. I never prayed, not once to ask God's favor on this marriage. I prayed over other things. I thought I was doing the right thing. When Daniel came into my life, I took for granted, that this was God's way of helping me out of my dilemma with Glen. How wrong I was. Now I needed God more than ever. When I felt abandoned by God, He let me know that I wasn't alone. When I least expected it, He showed up.

A few days later, Daniel called to let me know that he contacted an attorney and filed divorce papers.

"Good," I replied. I was elated. Thank God, I thought.

I called Johnny and Jill to tell them I was finally out of the house. I explained to them the straw that broke the camel's back.

"Our offer still stands. You can move in here with us," they said.

"It would be easier for Janel to go to school there and I would be close to my job."

"Don't worry about Daniel. He's not going to come around here and bother you," Johnny said.

I made arrangements to move in with them. I didn't want to tote a lot of baggage with me so I stored most of my belongings in my mothers' basement.

The weekend came. I was back in Philadelphia talking with my girlfriend, Margie. I told her what happened between Daniel and I. She offered to accompany me to Jersey to pick up the rest of my belongings from the house.

"Thank you for wanting to come with me, Margie. I feel much better not having to make the drive alone," I said.

"Oh, you know me, I got your back. I'm not going to let you do this alone. Let's go."

Margie and I hopped into the car and headed for Jersey. Along the way I told her we needed to stop at the police station for an escort. When we arrived there, two officers followed us to the house. I pulled my key from my pocket and opened the door. Daniel was home at the time. One officer stood guard in the bedroom and the other was in the living room talking with Margie. I pulled the rest of my belongings from the dresser and closet. The officer reminded me that I could only take my things and nothing the both of us accumulated during the marriage.

"I'm fine with that. I only want what's mine," I replied.

Once I had the rest of my things, Margie helped me load up the car.

When we got in the car, we realized it was so much stuff in the back, I could barely see out the rear window. I got out and rearranged the things so my visibility wasn't blocked.

We started laughing as we pulled off. The police officers left when they were assured I wouldn't be re-entering the house.

Margie and I headed back to Philadelphia, laughing all the way. She was the one I relied on to lift my spirits. I would go and sit with her and her mother for hours at a time in their home and talk about life in general, the goodness of God and how He moved spiritually in our lives. We helped each other by drawing on one another's strengths.

CHAPTER 8

It was September 1978. Janel was starting first grade. Daniel and I discussed where she should attend school and we both agreed that Jersey would be the better area. Janel and I moved in with Johnny and Jill. A few months later, I discovered that Jill was pregnant with her third child. I knew I had to find a place soon. Meanwhile, we adjusted to our temporary surroundings.

Every weekend, Janel and I went to stay with her grandmother. Being in Philadelphia on Sundays gave me the opportunity to attend church, once again, on a regular basis.

After the Christmas holidays were over, I searched for apartments to rent. I wanted to be centrally located between Janel's school and my workplace. I filled out numerous applications but was rejected each time. I was told my income was too low. I quickly became frustrated; first a failed marriage, then the inability to move forward on my own.

In early March 1979, Daniel called to invite me over for dinner. He was very pleasant, unlike the attitude he exhibited during our marriage. I was a little hesitant at first and didn't understand the invitation. He informed me that he just wanted to talk. I consented.

Two days later I arrived at Daniel's. He had the kitchen table set. Nice goblets adorned the table.

"I made you all of your favorites," he smiled.

Daniel was a great cook, much better than I. He worked in the galley when he was stationed in the Coast Guard. He knew how to cook for a large number of people. Daniel pulled out baked potatoes and lobster tails from the oven. He served Asti Spumante sparkling wine to compliment the meal. Daniel and I made small talk as we dined.

"This is quite a dish. What's the occasion for such a fancy feast?" I asked.

"I thought you might want me to drop the divorce proceedings. We still have time to change our minds before everything is finalized," he said.

"No Daniel. I don't want to change my mind. Let the divorce proceed as planned. I tried everything in my power to make our marriage work. I failed. We failed. I think we should cut our losses and move on."

"Okay," Daniel responded. "I just thought you might have had a change of heart."

"Daniel, let's not forget, you're the one who filed for the divorce two days after I left the house. Anyway, thanks for dinner. It was very thoughtful of you, but I must get going."

I arose to leave. Daniel got up and walked me to the door.

"Thanks again. I appreciated it very much," I said.

"Well, thanks for coming. I enjoyed your company."

I walked back to Jill's house. When I entered the house Jill quizzed me.

"What did Daniel want?"

"He wanted to see if I was willing to allow him to call off the divorce proceedings. He cooked lobster tails and baked potatoes. He also served Asti Spumante sparkling wine," I replied.

"He did what?" Jill laughed.

"Yes," I nodded.

A week later, the divorce became final. For the first time in my life, I felt like a heavy weight had been lifted from my shoulders.

In the coming weeks as Jill's pregnancy progressed, I was reminded that I needed to leave. They needed their space for the new baby. Jill said she was due in July. Much of April and May, I spent filling out more applications for apartments.

In June when school let out for the summer, I moved out of Johnny and Jill's house. I took Janel to my mother's house in Philadelphia to spend the summer. The commute back and forth to work was longer but I anticipated on finding something soon. In the meantime I continued to search for apartments. I continued to be rejected. I put it in God's hands because I couldn't do it on my own. Just when I was about to give up, I made one last effort to apply for another apartment. To my surprise, I was accepted. I leaped for joy. I was so happy that someone said yes to me, I cried.

During the summer, Rev. Williams had started a prison ministry. He told me that he had received a letter from Glen requesting a visit from him. In the letter he asked that I accompany him.

"He wants me to visit him and bring you along," he said.

"I don't know what for. I don't have any reason to want to see him."

"You shouldn't feel that way."

"Well, I do. After everything he has done to me, why would I want to go? Write him back and tell him I have no intention of coming. He needs to apologize for what he has done. Until then, I don't have anything to say."

Evidently, Rev. Williams relayed the message because the next correspondence indicated his willingness to apologize. I then decided I would go and listen to what he had to say.

When we arrived at the prison, Glen greeted us in the visiting area. He sat opposite us. I sat there unemotional, very quietly, waiting. Glen turned his attention to me.

"I apologize to you. The reason I did what I did is because, no woman has ever told me no."

"Well, there's always a first time. That is no excuse. You put me through hell and for what, because you couldn't stand rejection? That doesn't make sense. Something is seriously wrong with you."

Glen lowered his head and became silent and I finally felt vindicated from all the shame I carried within my being all those years.

Once outside the prison gates, I turned to Rev. Williams and said.

"I won't be coming back here. I'm glad I finally know why he did what he did but that wasn't a sincere apology. I got the answer I needed."

In September 1979, I moved into my apartment. I didn't really like the place but it was all I could afford at the time. Money was so tight, I couldn't buy any furniture. Janel and I sat on the floor Indian style and ate. There was a mattress on the bedroom floor for us to share. Jill gave me some curtains she no longer used to hang at the windows. Janel had a sad expression on her face. I knew she wasn't happy living in an empty apartment. I tried to console her and promised things would get better soon. I was ashamed of my empty apartment and I wouldn't invite any of my friends over, except for Margie. She understood how I felt and she would boost my spirit by joking around and making me laugh. She made me see the humorous side of my bad situation. When I was alone, I became very melancholy and I literally cried. I had no idea that being single again would be so hard. Notwithstanding, I was determined to push forward and make a way somehow. I prayed to God often, hoping He would hear my constant prayers.

One day I was out driving around, getting familiar with the area when I saw a sign at an apartment complex that read, Condos for sale. I slowed down and pulled into the complex and looked around at the units. Next, I went into the office to look at the model apartment. It was much nicer than what I had. I will never be able to afford one of these, I thought. I really liked the condo and I wished that I could get one of them. The receptionist at the desk suggested I fill out a form to see if I qualify.

"Okay," I said, "but I don't know. I'm not going to get my hopes up."

I returned to my dismal looking, lonely apartment. I turned the key in the lock and pushed the door open. Stepping into emptiness, I hurriedly slammed the door behind me. I was hungry so I headed for the kitchen. When I had finished cooking, I grabbed a plate from the cabinet. Then I spun around. There was no table to set the plate on. I sat cross-legged on the floor to eat. The tears rolled down my cheeks and dripped in little spots on the floor. I was a highly emotional person and cried often. The emptiness of this wide open space consumed me. As badly as I was treated by Daniel, I had to wonder, should I have stayed.

Daniel and I had made arrangements for Janel to finish school in Palmyra. I would drop Janel off at school in the morning. She would walk to Daniel's after school and wait for me to pick her up on my way home from work. She had Jill's kids to play with and keep her occupied until I got there.

One day on my routine stop to pick up Janel, Daniel said he had some mail for me. He said it's from the Postal Service. I reached out to accept the letter.

"Oh, thanks. This is probably another one of those letters they send every year asking if you wish to remain on the list for employment. They have sent two already. This is the third one," I said. I shoved the letter in my pocket and gathered up Janel's book bag.

"Okay, sweetie, let's go home."

"Mommy, what are we having for dinner tonight?"

"Your favorite dish of course, spaghetti."

Janel danced around with delight.

After dinner, Janel sat in the bedroom and watched television while I sat in the corner and opened my letter from the postal service. The letter stated that a position was available. I had a date and time to report for the interview. The phone number was printed at the bottom for confirmation.

I arrived promptly at the post office at the appointed time and knocked at the postmaster's door. I was offered a clerk position because there wasn't an opening for letter carrier. I remembered when I took the test, I checked the block for letter carrier craft. I wasn't sure what the clerk position entailed. At the conclusion of the interview I was given a start date of October 18th. I was so excited. Finally, I managed to get my foot in the door of the United States Postal Service. Hallelujah.

A week later, I heard from the Condo sales office. They wanted me to verify my current salary status.

"I'm between jobs, right now. I will be starting a new job with the U.S. Postal Service in a week."

"Okay, that shouldn't be a problem. What will be your starting salary?"

I told them. At the conclusion of the phone call they told me it was a good possibility that I might qualify to purchase the apartment. They said they would get back to me. In the meantime, I called Western Union to give them notice of my resignation. When the call came, they told me I had qualified to make the purchase. I was so happy, I kissed the floor. Finally, things were looking up for me. I felt I was on my way to becoming financially stable. Nothing but the goodness of God made this possible. What a blessing!

I couldn't wait to drag my few belongings and Janel's things into the new condo. When she saw it, she was thrilled. It was a beautiful thing to see my little girl's eyes light up. It was a one bedroom apartment, so I bought a fold up cot for Janel and placed it in the living room. I still didn't have any furniture. I didn't care. I had the condo.

A month later, I stopped at Daniel's to pick up Janel when I ran into Lionel and Lydia.

"How are you doing?" Lydia asked.

"I'm better, thank you."

"It's been a while since we've seen you."

"Yeah, I know. I'm living in Burlington Township now. I just bought a condo but I need to furnish it."

"You know what? You're in luck. I can help. I have furniture I need to get rid of. Lionel and I are moving to Washington State because of his job. We can't take this stuff with us. I need to get rid of a lot of things. Come on in and I'll show you what I have."

I followed Lydia into her house. She had a lovely living room set. It was a beautiful, brown plaid material with a wooden frame. She also had a bedroom and kitchen set. All the pieces looked fairly new.

"You can have all three sets for a hundred dollars."

"Really, that's wonderful. I'll take it," I replied enthusiastically.

A few days later, all of the furniture was delivered to me. It looked fantastic in the condo. I had everything I needed. God had blessed me again. How grateful I was.

Once the condo purchase went through, all kinds of credit card offers were pouring in. I was finally getting back on my feet after such a difficult time. The blessings were truly flowing in my life.

It was October, 1980. I transferred Janel to the new school in our area. She was very happy and liked it a lot. I was glad she was able to adjust so well. With my new job, my schedule changed almost daily. There were times when I couldn't be home with Janel in the mornings. I didn't like leaving my little girl alone. She was eight years old. I worried constantly when I had to work the early morning hours. I trained my child to be a successful latch key kid. I thanked God for giving me an obedient child. I laid her clothes out for her each evening. All she had to do was get dressed. She took her baths at night. I left her cereal on the kitchen table. I reminded her to remember to put the milk back in the refrigerator. I left her lunch money in her book bag. Every morning I called her to make sure she was okay. I instructed her never to answer the door if anyone knocked or rang the bell. My little girl followed my instructions exactly. She walked to the bus stop with her friends she had met in the complex. The good news was, the children didn't have to cross any streets to get to the bus. For the next five years, my child would remain a latch key kid. God kept Janel safe the entire time.

It was early 1982, about fifteen months since moving into my condo. The telephone rang. I picked it up.

"Hello," I answered.

The voice on the other end startled me. It was Glen. I became annoyed. After all I had done to escape him he found a way to contact me. Worse than that, he was released from prison.

"Why are you calling here?" I demanded.

"I think I am in a better position to take care of Janel than you are. I have a good paying job now."

"How much money do you make?" I asked.

When he told me, I cracked a smile.

"First of all, you lost your parental rights years ago. Secondly, you don't make more money than I do. Goodbye Glen."

I slammed the phone down. I didn't need this nightmare coming back to haunt me. For several minutes I paced the floor trying to figure out my next move. He had my number, now I wondered how long it would be before he showed up at my door.

I called Mrs. Phillips and told her about Glen. I related how I didn't feel safe with him walking the streets again.

"Come to Philly. I have something for you. He won't come anywhere near you," she promised.

A few days later, I stopped by Mrs. Phillips' house. She had gathered some green leaves which I couldn't identify and told me to lay it across my doorstep.

"What is this?" I asked.

"Don't worry about what it is. He will not step foot across your door. I guarantee it," she insisted.

She never identified that plant. I took it home and did as I was told. Glen never showed up at my residence.

A week later I was seated in church for the morning worship service. I sat in the pew at the rear of the church next to the last row. When the late worshippers were admitted, Glen walked in and entered the row directly in front of me. I stared in disbelief. I couldn't believe he had the gall to show up here.

During the call to discipleship, Glen rose from his seat and walked down the aisle to the front of the sanctuary. He stood before the pastor. Rev. Williams extended his hand. A feeling of uneasiness swept over me. When the service ended, I approached the pastor's study. I knocked at the door. Rev. Williams opened it, allowing me to enter.

"If Glen returns for the Right Hand of Fellowship, I will be forced to leave this church. Out of all the churches in the city of Philadelphia, he had to pick this one. This is just another deceitful act to harass me. He's not serious about God. He's playing games."

Rev. Williams assured me that he probably wouldn't come back.

It was June 1982. School was out of session for the summer. Janel looked forward to spending her vacation in Philadelphia with her grandmother. My mother was just as happy to have her only granddaughter around. Even though Janel spent weekends with her throughout the year, she hoped that we both would move back to Philadelphia eventually. That wasn't in the cards for me. I preferred the Jersey lifestyle.

I had the freedom to socialize with my friends. I needed an outlet. I wanted to keep my mind off the past and concentrate on other things. I had bouts of loneliness from time to time. At some point, I had a brief affair which resulted in another pregnancy. I vented my frustration to a very good friend of mine. I told her I wanted an abortion but didn't have the money. She offered to help and gave me her DPA card and told me to use it. She explained that the procedure wouldn't cost anything. I told her I appreciated it but I didn't think it was a good idea. She persuaded me to take it, since I didn't have any other alternative. I thanked her and set everything in motion. I entered the hospital under an assumed name. Once there, I had to remember to answer to her name and not mine. I repeated her name over and over again in my head so that I wouldn't forget. It was the craziest thing I ever did. Suppose something went wrong? I could have died in that hospital and no one would've known my true identity. Once again, God pulled me through to see another day. I thought to myself, never again would I pull a stupid stunt like that.

I had many moments of sadness throughout my young adult years. In those moments I had made many bad decisions. I held Glen accountable for every bad thing that went wrong in my life. I blamed him for my abortions as well as all the other crazy choices I had made. I resented him for impinging upon my self-worth. He vowed to turn my daughter against me. My heart carried the burden, a burden which I couldn't let go and give to God. Matthew 6:14-15 says – "If you forgive those who sin against you, your heavenly Father will forgive you. But if you refuse to forgive others, your Father will not forgive your sins." I read the verses over and over. The tears flooded my eyes. I said to myself, maybe someday and somehow. I can't do it now.

For several weeks, I brooded over the abortions. Because I was pro-choice in my decisions regarding abortion, I felt it necessary to go the route I had taken. That is not to say that I didn't feel bad about my choices, because I did.

Late October 1982, I started dating again. This time it was different. I decided I would date only married men. I was very angry on the inside. I wanted control of the relationship. When I was tired of looking at them, I told them to go home. If I didn't want them around, I told them to stay away. If I needed money, I asked for it. A married man could be putty in my hands, if I chose to do so. It was never my intention to break up their relationship with their wives. I was in the relationship for one reason only, and that was to satisfy myself.

After five years in the condo, I decided I wanted to buy a house. I needed a change of scenery. I shopped around with a real estate agent, looking at several different houses. Nothing seemed to satisfy me completely. Eventually I got tired of trampling around from one to another. I finally decided on a house. After I had settled in about six months later, I decided I didn't really like the house that much. I remained there one year, before putting it on the market. I wasn't in the place long enough to build any equity. Janel didn't seem to be that thrilled with it either. She stayed in Philadelphia every chance she got. During the summer months I was alone in the house. It was pretty quiet and depressing. When the sale went through, I didn't make a profit. I got back exactly what it cost me for a year's worth of mortgage payments. I had to pay points because I sold it to a vet. I had to replace the hot water tank because it had a crack in it. Actually, it was the responsibility of the previous owners to replace the tank. I believed they sold the house to me knowing the crack was there. I was disappointed with how they got over. You live and you learn. That's life.

In 1986, I moved back to my mother's house. She was thrilled to have us back with her and we were thrilled to be back. I decided I wanted to travel and see a little of the world. Now I had the money to do so.

I was watching television one day when I saw a commercial about the starving children in third world countries. I've seen it many times before. This particular time, I paid more attention to it. It touched my heart. Every day in the Unites States, food is wasted. When I think about the people who don't have anything to eat, it's heartbreaking. I thought about how good it was to live in the United States. I decided to sign up and sponsor a child. I joined Plan International and anxiously awaited my info packet on the child I had chosen. Her name was Kasarna and she was from Indonesia. When the package arrived I was captivated by the beautiful little girl's eyes. She was so adorable, standing in front of her house alongside her mother. I was overwhelmed with joy. We started corresponding back and forth through letters. Each time I received a letter, I stopped whatever I was doing to open and read it. One day I told myself, "I want to meet my sponsored child."

CHAPTER 9

In August 1987, my oldest sister-in-law, Christine sponsored a four day cruise from her church. Every year or so, she spearheaded trips to many interesting places. I mentioned the trip to Dee-Dee. She was excited about it and decided to accompany me. We boarded the Amtrak train to Miami. When we arrived at the Port of Miami, I glanced up at the ship. It wasn't the largest of ships, but it was beautiful. We boarded the ship and quickly found our cabin. We were told that the luggage would arrive later.

Dee-Dee and I entered the cabin and glanced around at our surroundings. We were pleased at the size of the room. It was big enough for two people to move around comfortably. When our luggage arrived we began to unpack.

A few hours later we felt the ship moving and realized we had left port. We were on our way to the Bahamas. It was my first time on a cruise ship and I found the experience exciting.

There was a knock at the door and Dee-Dee went to open it. The cabin steward came to greet us and welcome us aboard. He introduced himself and assured us if we needed anything, to just call and he would be nearby. We thanked him and he left. A few minutes later Dee-Dee walked into the bathroom and discovered we didn't have enough shower caps.

"Gerri, holler down the hall for the cabin steward and tell him what we need."

"Okay, what's his name?" I asked.

"He just introduced himself."

"Sorry, I wasn't really paying attention."

Dee-Dee leaned over my shoulder and pulled a name card from the slot holder on the door.

"Dian," she said.

I opened the door and stepped into the corridor.

"Dian," I called.

I stood there a few seconds. When he didn't appear, I shut the door and returned to my unpacking.

Ten minutes later, Dian appeared and Dee-Dee requested more shower caps.

"I'll be right back," he said.

Several minutes later, a light tap on the door indicated that Dian had returned. Dee-Dee answered the door. I looked up as he entered. For the first time, I actually noticed him. I thought he was so cute. He was very polite and had nice physical features. I felt an instant attraction to him. I struck up a conversation with him for a few minutes. The more I talked, the more I felt drawn to him.

"Where are you from, Dian?" I asked.

"Indonesia," he said.

"Oh how wonderful. I have a foster child that I sponsor from Indonesia. I am planning a trip there next summer to meet her."

"That is so nice. You will like Indonesia."

"I'm looking forward to it. Will you be there when I get there?"

"No, I won't. I will be in Saudi Arabia at that time. "I'm making a pilgrimage to Mecca."

He explained how Muslims who are physically and financially able are required to make the trip at least once in their lifetime. When Dian left the room, I turned to Dee-Dee.

"He is so handsome," I said.

"Girl, you are so crazy." Dee-Dee laughed.

"Yeah, I might be, but I'm single and I can look if I want to."

"Yes, you certainly can," she averred.

I picked up the activity sheet and perused it carefully.

"There are a lot of nice things to do aboard ship and outside tours to take. We're going to have four days of fun and excitement," I exclaimed.

Dee-Dee glanced at the sheet I was holding. We planned our agenda for the evening.

"After dinner, let's go to the entertainment show," I suggested.

"Okay, that sounds like a winner," Dee-Dee replied.

When the show ended, Dee-Dee decided to retire to the cabin. I wanted to familiarize myself with the ship, so I walked the corridors for over an hour, taking note of where everything was located. Eventually I headed back to my room.

The next morning, our cabin door was ajar. Dian knocked on the door and poked his head in.

"Good morning ladies. If there is anything you need, please let me know."

"Okay, we will," I responded with a smile.

Later in the afternoon I was standing in the area of the photographer. Several people were lining up for photographs. Dian was working nearby.

"Dian, will you take a picture with me?"

"Oh, I can't do that without permission. You could ask my boss."

"Well, where do I find him?"

"He's right over there," pointing to the other side of the room.

His boss stood to one side of the room talking with staff officers. I walked over to him to ask if Dian could take a picture with me and he granted permission. I waved to Dian to come over. After the pictures were taken, Dian ran off to finish his work.

Dee-Dee and I spent the rest of the day taking a tour around Freeport. That evening we hit the casinos. Dee-Dee wasn't much of a gambler so it didn't hold her interest for long. On the other hand, I loved playing the slot machines and remained there for an hour. Dee-Dee walked off and said she would return shortly. After losing several times I decided to call it quits. I glanced at my watch. Dee-Dee had not yet returned. I decided to go to the cabin to see if she was there.

On my way back, I ran into Dian. We talked for a while. He asked me if I would go to a disco club with him the following night. Of course I said yes. When I reached the cabin, I found Dee-Dee inside. I told her Dian asked me to go out with him.

The next morning Dee-Dee and I took a shore excursion of Nassau. In the evening I prepared for my date with Dian. I was so excited he asked me out. I hurried down the gang plank. Dian was standing on the pier waving at Dee-Dee.

"Take good care of Gerri," Dee-Dee warned.

"I will. Everything will be fine," he promised.

We grabbed a cab and hurried off. First we decided to go to a restaurant and eat dinner. Later inside the disco, we found a table and sat down. The music was too loud for me. The waitress came over to us and asked what we would like to drink. Dian ordered a coke. I wrote on a napkin my choice of drink and handed it to her. The music was so loud I couldn't hear myself talk.

"Gerri, do you want to leave?" Dian asked.

"No, it's okay. I'll adjust to the noise level."

We looked around the room. The place was full of people. He asked me to dance. I refused. The very next record the disc jockey played was my favorite love song. I looked at Dian. I had changed my mind.

"Yes Dian. I do want to dance."

He led me onto the dance floor. He wrapped his arms around my shoulders. I rested my head in his chest as we slow danced to the beautiful love song. When the music stopped, we were staring into each other's eyes. Dian leaned in to kiss me. It was a warm beautiful moment we shared, a moment I wanted to hold onto forever. As we returned to our table, people nearby were staring at us. I didn't care. I was in my own world at that moment, sharing it with Dian.

Back at the ship, he stopped short and stood on the pier.

"I can't accompany you back to your cabin door. I am not allowed to fraternize with the passengers."

"It's okay Dian. I'm aware of the rules."

"Did you have a nice time tonight?"

"Of course I did, and you also, right?"

"Yes, I enjoyed it very much," he said.

"Tomorrow the ship sails for home and I'm not ready to leave," I whined.

"I will see you before you go," he promised.

When I entered the cabin I found Dee-Dee packing her suitcase.

"Did you and Dian have a nice time?" she asked.

The smile on my face answered her question.

"Uh oh, looks like you are falling in love," she mused.

"Maybe, I'm just sorry we have to leave tomorrow. We had a lot of fun. This trip was too short. I like cruising a lot. I am going to do this more often," I said.

Early the next morning, Dian appeared at the door. Dee-Dee turned to look as he entered.

"I'm going down the hall to give you two a few private moments," she said.

Dee-Dee hurried out and Dian shut the door behind her.

"Are you going to come back? I hope to see you again."

"I don't want to leave you behind. I promise I will be back." I said.

"When will that be?"

"I'll be back in six months. Maybe I'll come during the week of Valentine's Day."

"What is Valentine's Day?" Dian asked.

"I'll explain it when I return." I will miss you a lot. Please write me."

I handed Dian my address and phone number.

"I will miss you too, Gerri, and I will write soon.

We embraced each other with a kiss. I found out that we intuitively sensed each other's character.

"Remember, don't ever change. I like you just the way you are. You have a beautiful heart Gerri."

"I like you too, Dian."

I stood there relishing his words he just quoted. No one has ever said anything like that to me before. It was so amazing. Here was a stranger I met only four days ago and he could see my heart. He gave me back my self-worth that was lost for so long. Once again, I began to feel like the person that I had always believed myself to be.

I caught a glimpse of sadness as he turned to leave. Evidently, he didn't want the moment to end either. Dian slowly turned the knob on the door and disappeared down the hall. I lingered in the doorway for a few seconds. My eyes filled with tears. Every special moment we spent together raced through my mind.

Several minutes later, Dee-Dee entered the cabin to retrieve her suitcase. With bags in hand, we exited the room. Periodically, I looked back as I descended the gang plank but Dian was nowhere in sight.

It was on this trip that I experienced the un-expectable—an in depth conversation with a (Muslim) staff person. It turned out to be what (M. Buber) calls an "I-Thou" experience in which persons are experienced as subjects in contrast to an "I-It" experience when persons are experienced as an object or thing. The dialogic relationship was for me cathartic, transformative and inspirational. The best way I can express it is in the following poem by Nixon Waterman:

> If I knew you and you knew me,
> If both of us could clearly see;
> And with an inner sight divine,
> The meaning of your heart and mine,
>
> I'm sure that we would differ less,
> And clasp our hands in friendliness;
> Our thoughts would pleasantly agree,
> If I knew you and you knew me.

Every day, I went to my post office box to look for a blue airmail envelope. I wondered how long it would take before I would hear from Dian. Two weeks after returning home, I received my first letter. My heart skipped a beat as I fondly recalled the memories we shared. I carefully opened the envelope and sat on a stool to read my letter. It was so exciting to read the words written on the paper despite Dian's difficulty with English. I tucked the letter away in my purse. When I got home, I re-read the letter again and again.

Over the next several months Dian and I wrote letters back and forth. I told him to call me by telephone when he wanted to get in touch right away. I received four letters and two phone calls during the time we were apart from each other. I was fantasizing about the moment we would meet again.

I was six years into my relationship with a married man (Miles) and as time went by my conscience bothered me more and more. He noticed the change in me when I returned from my cruise. I let him know I had met someone else I was attracted to and he wasn't happy about it. I had to remind him that I was the single one in this relationship and that I could decide to leave at any point in time. I told him of my plans to return to the ship. He told me if I left, he wouldn't be waiting for me when I got back.

Valentine's week, 1988, I boarded a plane headed for Miami. This was my first flight. I was a little apprehensive about flying. I wasn't sure I would like it, plus I would be flying alone. If I wanted to see Dian again I had to gather up enough nerve to get on the plane. I convinced myself it was a piece of cake. Once the plane was in the air, I started to relax. I sat back and enjoyed the flight. I forgot all about my personal problems for a while.

During the six months correspondence, Dian informed me what cabin to choose so that he would have easy access to visiting me. I had a choice of two cabins. At the time of booking, only one remained available. I made sure it had my name on it.

Now I stood on the pier, looking up, anxiously awaiting a glimpse of Dian, but he didn't appear. The boarding line was long. As I slowly neared the gang plank, I occasionally glanced up. Some of the cabin stewards stood around greeting the passengers and directing them where they needed to go. When I reached the top, I checked in and hurriedly looked for my room. Upon entering the cabin, I found a fruit basket on the table and a gift box of champagne glasses. Beside the gifts laid a small white envelope. Inside there was an invitation to the captain's private cocktail party. I felt special, indeed.

That's nice, I thought. I glanced around the cabin, very satisfied with the size of my accommodations. I immediately felt right at home.

Once my bags arrived, I started to unpack. There was a knock at the door. When I opened it, the cabin steward stood there. He introduced himself and told me if I needed anything to just call. I continued breaking down my bags. About twenty minutes later, I heard a light tap on the door.

"Come in," I called out.

Dian stood in the door with a huge smile on his face. He entered, quickly closing the door behind him. He was dressed differently. He no longer wore the cabin steward attire. Dian was quite handsome in his new uniform. He had become a staff officer.

"Gerri, I am so happy to see you again. Welcome back."

"Good to see you too. I've missed you so much. I like your new uniform."

Dian took me in his arms and kissed me. I clung to him for several seconds.

"Wait right here, Gerri. I will be back in a moment."

Dian left the room and returned as fast as he had left. In his hands he carried a bottle of champagne wrapped in a towel.

"Wow, for me? I'm impressed."

He sat the bottle down on the table. We conversed a few more minutes.

"Enjoy the champagne, Gerri." I have to leave for now, but I will return later."

He quickly kissed me good-bye and was out the door.

I sat on the edge of my bed, glancing over the itinerary. I placed a check mark next to the items that interested me. It was an open seating for dinner the first night. I had eaten the few snacks I brought with me and was ready for a delicious, mouth-watering meal. I opened the door to my cabin because I felt a little shut in. The voices of other passengers could be heard as they moved to and fro.

My cabin steward reappeared in the doorway to check on me. He struck up a conversation and I got the impression he was trying to come on to me. I told him I wasn't interested. Dian returned and entered the room. The steward hid behind the door as Dian advanced towards me. I tried to signal Dian that he was there. I didn't want him to say or do anything that would give away our relationship. Fortunately, Dian must have sensed his presence. He turned around and saw him standing against the wall hiding behind the door. He looked back at me.

"We will talk later," he said.

Dian glanced at the steward once more, and headed for the door.

I turned my attention to the steward.

"It's time for you to leave."

"Dian," I called to him. "Please, take him with you."

Embarrassed, the steward followed him out of the room.

I walked over to the night stand and marveled at the beautiful champagne glasses. I carefully removed one of them from the box to get a closer look. Etched in the glass was a dolphin. They were very delicate and so beautiful. I didn't want to break it. I carefully returned the glass to the box and sat it down on the table. I smiled with satisfaction at the lovely gifts I received. I hurriedly changed clothes and headed for the dining room. I was so hungry and looked forward to a scrumptious meal.

It felt strange to be traveling alone without a roommate. I knew I had to fill the time with a lot of things from the itinerary because Dian didn't have a lot of time to spend with me. I planned to settle for whatever time I could get with him. Later that evening, Dian asked me to explain what Valentine's Day was.

"It's a long story of how Valentine's Day originated. I will tell you the short side of it. Valentine's Day is a special day for the romantic at heart. It's a day for sending greeting cards, giving gifts such as flowers or candy to loved ones," I explained. "Do you understand, Dian?"

"Yes I think so. You are very special to me, Gerri."

"Thank you. I feel the same way about you, Dian," I said smiling.

As we conversed, Dian explained that our meetings would be sporadic because of his busy schedule. I told him I was willing to work around his schedule.

"I have been to a lot of these activities the first time I was here. My main focus is you. I will go to other things when you can't be here," I said.

Dian wanted to make sure that I would enjoy my trip.

"Dian, don't worry about that," I assured him. In my spare time I will find something to do."

"Okay, Gerri. It's important that you have a nice time."

"I promise. I'll be just fine."

He rested his hand on my shoulder. "I have to go now but I will be back later when I get a chance."

"Okay, I'll be here," I responded.

As Dian rose to leave, I reached for the activity sheet and glanced over it. There wasn't really anything that I couldn't miss. I quickly donned my sleepwear and laid down on my bed to relax. I closed my eyes as the waves gently beat against the ship. Before I knew it, morning had dawned.

I showered and dressed for my 6:00 a.m. breakfast. The dining room was practically empty except for a few early risers like myself. Breakfast was the best meal of the day to get me started and I didn't mind getting up early. I lingered on the upper decks for most of the morning. When I returned to my room, I found that my cabin steward had been there. My pajamas were neatly twisted into a beautiful design, lying atop my well made-up bed.

Hmmm, nice, that's pretty creative, I thought.

I waited for an hour to see if Dian would show up. When he didn't appear I started to become restless. I had no way of contacting him, so, waiting was my only option. I began to pace the floor a while until I decided to leave the cabin. I slowly made my way to the gift shop and browsed around. Next I stopped at the bar and ordered a Bahama Mama, one of my favorite island drinks, before heading to the casino. When I got tired of the slots, I walked up and down the corridors of the ship hoping to run into Dian. Eventually, I found him. His back was turned and he didn't see me approaching.

"Hello, Dian."

He whirled around.

"Hi, Gerri, did you sleep well last night?"

"Just like a baby," I replied.

Dian's dark eyes sparkled as he smiled. "That's good. I'm sorry I didn't get a chance to see you this morning."

"That's okay. I know you are very busy."

"I'll see you later this evening," he whispered.

Dian touched my hand gently then hurried off. I watched him as he disappeared down the corridor.

Once back in my cabin, I reached for the activity schedule to find what interested me. Glancing over the itinerary, I decided to take an island tour the next morning. I would be back in time to possibly see Dian once his work was done. I tried to stay engaged with different activities so I wouldn't become bored. The casino would hold my attention for long periods of time. I decided to head back to the casino. As luck would have it, I won some money. I fanned the twenties in my hand as I climbed the stairs to the next level. As I reached the top of the stairs, I ran into Dian. I quickly shoved the money into my pocket. I didn't know how he felt about gambling and I didn't want to take the chance. I didn't know anything about the Muslim faith so I was on my guarded behavior.

"Hi, Gerri, what have you been up to this evening?"

"Oh not much, just roaming around the ship." I replied.

"I hope you are really having a good time, Gerri."

"Don't worry, Dian. Everything is fine."

"Okay. Have you been to the casino, yet?" he asked.

I had to wonder if he saw me put the money in my pocket. "Oh yes. I've been there."

"Be careful, Gerri. Don't lose too much of your money," he warned.

"Oh, I won't. I don't gamble like that," I assured him.

One of the cabin stewards passed by and started speaking to Dian in a foreign language. I was surprised to discover that Dian was speaking Spanish. When the steward had disappeared down the hall, he turned his attention back to me.

"I didn't realize you spoke Spanish, Dian."

"Yes, I speak five languages."

"Which ones do you speak?" I asked.

"Well, I speak my native language, Bahasa Indonesia, French, Italian, Spanish and English. I guess you can tell that I struggle with English, but I'm trying to speak it better so that you will understand everything I say."

"You are doing great with the English."

"Really, Gerri, it sounds okay to you?"

"Of course, it does Dian. Don't worry. I understand everything you say."

Once in a while Dian struggled with words. He thought his broken words bothered me but I convinced him that wasn't true.

"I will see you later, Gerri. Get some rest. You look a little tired."

"I promise I will rest. I'll see you later."

After a hearty breakfast the next morning, I prepared for my island tour. I spent the best part of the day off the ship. As the afternoon wore on, I started to become anxious. I wanted to see Dian. I couldn't wait to get back to the ship. Time was passing quickly and it would soon be time to go home. I wanted more time with Dian. Later in the evening, he showed up at my cabin door.

"I only have a few minutes before I have to leave. I have some things I have to do."

"Are you coming back later?" I asked. "Dian, I think we should spend more time together."

"Gerri, I don't know if I can do that. I will try."

I was falling deeper and deeper for Dian and I wanted him to know it. I wasn't sure whether he would be back or not. I sat on the edge of my bed and pondered where, if anywhere, this relationship was going. Realistically speaking, I knew it couldn't develop any further than right here and now. There were too many cultural and religious differences between the two of us. For us, it was like being suspended in time, blocking out the rest of the world. Neither one of us seem to care about the differences for the moment. We both enjoyed each other's company.

I looked over at the beautiful fruit basket which sat on the table. The fruit looked so inviting. I reached for an apple. I bit into the fruit and it was very sweet and tasty. Next, I reached for a pear. I poured a small amount of the sparkling wine into a small glass. The wine trickled down my throat. I savored the delicate, sweet taste as my mind reminisced over the encounters with Dian.

Later that evening, I sat in my cabin, hoping I would hear from Dian soon. As I continued to savor more wine, there was a knock at the door. I quickly opened it. There he was, uniform in hand.

"Come in quickly, Dian."

"Gerri, I took a big risk coming here."

"Don't worry. As far as I'm concerned, no one will ever know that you were here."

Dian seemed to relax at my words of assurance.

We had a meaningful conversation.

"Gerri, I am very nervous right now. I could lose my job if anyone finds out."

"You don't have to worry about that. No one will find you here."

Dian reached for me and gently kissed me. I fell asleep in his arms. In the early morning hours, Dian jumped up to report to work.

"Gerri, I must leave now."

He quickly kissed me goodbye and said he would see me later. Dian peeked up and down the corridor. The way was clear so he hurried out the door.

I laid awake for a while before falling back into a tranquil sleep. It was Valentine's Day, the best Valentine's Day I have ever had. It was special because I shared it with Dian.

Returning to my cabin after breakfast, I ran into Dian standing on the deck. He told me his boss questioned him as to his whereabouts last night and he said he couldn't sleep and was out on the deck all night. We agreed to catch up with each other later.

I felt contented. For once, my life seemed complete in the moment. All day long, my thoughts were on Dian. There wasn't any room for anything else in my head, not even my boyfriend I had left back home. Dian filled every space in my mind and heart.

For the first time, I began seriously to raise questions about the meaning of life, the purpose of living, and more specifically, God's purpose for my life. For the first time, I had peace within which – in the language of the New Testament – "passeth all understanding."

In the evening, many passengers were lined up to take photos. I thought of Dian. This was a special night and I wanted to get a picture with him in his new uniform. He was so handsome with his emblems and stripes running across his shoulders. I stood off to the side watching others take photographs in their beautiful outfits. I waited a long time. Finally, Dian passed through the area.

"Dian," I called out to him.

He came over to where I was standing.

"I want you to take a picture with me."

"Okay, give me a minute. I will be right back," he said.

A few minutes later, he returned. We took the picture. The next morning the pictures were on display. I went to the photo lobby area to look for the photograph. For several minutes I searched but it wasn't amongst the rest.

Later, back at the cabin, a light tap was heard at the door. I swung it open to find Dian standing there. He had the photograph of us in his hand.

"I'm so glad you have the picture. I looked for a long time but couldn't find it. Thank you, Dian. I was worried."

I stared at the photo of the two of us. Oh how beautiful it was.

"Do you like the picture, Dian?'

"Yes, I do."

"Do you want to keep it?" I asked.

'No Gerri, I want you to have it."

I reached for him and kissed him.

"Thanks for bringing it to me."

"You are welcome, Gerri."

Dian took me by the hand.

"You have been so kind to me. I am glad that we met. I love you, Gerri."

"I love you too. I wish that tomorrow would never come. It's time to go home again. I could become a stowaway aboard this ship."

He laughed.

"Gerri, I know it's hard to say goodbye. Hopefully, we will meet again."

"Dian, leave this ship and come home with me."

"I wish I could, but I can't."

Dian and I held each other tight for several minutes. Tears started to form in my eyes.

"Gerri, please don't cry."

Dian wiped the tears from my cheeks as they ran down my face. He cupped my chin in his hand as he leaned over to kiss me. I was swept with emotion as I clung to him.

Once Dian was gone, I started packing my bags, knowing that tomorrow morning would be the last time I would see him. Aware that I had fallen in love, was breaking my heart, that this huge separation would one day, become a distant memory. It was the longest night I had to endure. I slept very little. In the morning I was very tired. I opened the door of the cabin, hoping that Dian would appear once more. I was stalling for time, knowing I had to exit the cabin very soon. Several minutes went by. Where was he? Wasn't he coming to say good-bye? Frustrated, I grabbed my luggage by the handle and started to roll it out the door, almost colliding into him.

"Dian, you finally showed up. I didn't think I was going to see you before leaving."

He stood in the doorway.

"I had to come to see you one more time, Gerri. It is hard for me to let go. I am going to miss you so much."

Dian stepped inside the cabin and closed the door.

"Gerri, I promise I will write you soon."

"I hope so, Dian."

We embraced each other one last time.

"Take care of yourself, Dian, and don't let any of those other women steal you from me."

"I love you, Gerri. I'm not interested in anyone else."

With one last kiss, we parted. When I turned around for a final sweep of the room, making sure I had packed everything, Dian had disappeared. For a moment I felt so lost. Finally, I mustered up enough courage and strength to put one foot in front of the other. I proceeded down the corridor to the gang plank, dabbing my eyes as I felt them mist. I never looked back.

Upon departing the ship at the end of the cruise, I recalled the words of the Negro spiritual, my good Lord done been there, blessed my soul and gone away. I felt healed by a heavenly angel.

CHAPTER 10

Once home, I focused my attention on the little girl in the photograph which I fostered from Plan International. So, this is Kasarna, my sponsored child. She captivated me with her small, dark, beady eyes and her short cut hairdo that molded her petite, round face. She was standing in front of her house with a slightly oversized dress on that fell just above her thin, dainty knees. On her feet she wore flip flop sandals, standing there so erect and still, her legs stretched in a V-shaped pose. I stared at the photograph that the agency had sent me. What a beautiful child, I thought, as the eyes gazed back at me. An inkling in my gut revealed to me I had to meet her face to face. I always wanted to travel afar and this was the perfect opportunity to do both.

In early March I decided to contact a travel agent to make my arrangements for traveling to Indonesia. My sister-in-law, Christine, recommended her travel agency because she had a good relationship in planning the church trips with him. I set up a meeting with the agent to work out an itinerary. I wanted to see different parts of Indonesia, so my stops included Jakarta, Yogyakarta and Bali. The total trip was nineteen days. The agent informed me that my departure date was good but I would be on standby for my return flight. He promised he would work hard to find me a flight home. I was due to leave the United States in July, which gave me four months. Certainly by then I believed a seat would open up for me.

As the weeks flew by I became more and more excited about my trip. My mother and my friends thought I was crazy for wanting to travel so far alone. At age thirty-four, I did things on a whim, just as I did when I was in my twenties. I was fearless. No one could talk me out of it. I was convinced that God would watch over me.

Finally the day arrived. I hurried to the airport, still on standby for a return flight. With the self-assurance that I would be alright, I pressed on. Upon checking in at the desk I found that my flight to California had been cancelled. There was no other flight leaving Philadelphia that day that would connect me to my overseas flight in time.

"What am I going to do now? I must get on a flight today," addressing the ticket agent.

"Mrs. Bryant, please do not panic. Let me see what I can do."

The ticket agent quickly checked other flight schedules that were possibly available.

"Okay, I don't have any domestic flights available going to the West Coast but I do have an international flight I can put you on. I can fly you on KLM but this flight will take you through Europe," she said.

"That's sounds like a plan. It won't cost anything more, will it?" I asked.

"No, you're fine. Here is the gate information and departure time. This flight is leaving soon, so I must work fast to get you on it."

The agent reprinted my ticket and handed it to me.

"Thank you so much. Anything that will get me in Indonesia on schedule is a blessing."

I gathered my carry-on and hurried towards the gate. Once safely aboard the plane, I sat down to relax and gather my thoughts. The flight was very nice and the food was good. The plane went through a storm with very little turbulence. I stepped off the plane in Jakarta, the capitol city, the next day. I was anxious to get settled in my hotel and just rest from my long flight.

The next morning I took a tour of Jakarta. I was in awe at the beautiful batik prints that were being dyed. The women sat making intricate patterns of beautiful garments, scarfs and quilts. I bought souvenirs to take home to family and friends.

The Amusement Park was exciting. There, I saw the tallest Indonesian on roller skates. He probably towered over six feet. I remember so vividly the seal that jumped up to kiss me and held on to my cheek for a few seconds before letting go. Nearby tourists who witnessed the incident were laughing and trying to aim their cameras for a shot.

I spent five days in Jakarta before moving on to Yogyakarta, where I would meet Kasarna.

I boarded Garuda Airlines for my flight to Yogyakarta. Upon landing, I headed for the Ambarrukmo Palace Hotel where I would stay for the next five days. The next day I took a tour of the Borobudur Temple, a popular tourist site for millions of visitors.

The following morning I arrived at the Plan Office where I met the staff. They explained to me how their community based development programs work. I was introduced to my interpreter who would be accompanying me on the trip.

Kasarna's village was three hours away. Periodically, we navigated tough terrain by jeep during the journey.

When we arrived at Kasarna's house, I took in the surrounding landscape. The grass and trees were thick around the yard in some spots while other areas were bare patches of dirt. A scrawny looking goat stood nearby feeding on something from the ground.

As we approached the house, a young woman pushed open the front door. She was clutching the hand of a little girl as they walked toward us; behind her, other family members followed. I soon learned that Kasarna's father wasn't amongst them. He was at work, therefore, I missed the opportunity to meet him.

My language interpreter stood next to me as we greeted each other. The little girl looked exactly as she did in the photo, wearing the same dress and flip flops. Her hair was sticking straight up on top where a rubber band held a small section of her hair. Her mother gave her an encouraging nudge and the child shook my hand and greeted me with a Japanese phrase of welcome. My sponsored child couldn't speak any English, nor could any of her relatives.

In my hand, I carried a large shopping bag. It was full of goodies which I had brought from the Unites States and locally after arriving in Yogyakarta.

Once inside the house, I quickly observed my surroundings. My eyes rested on the coffee table in front of the sofa which held a large platter of native snacks and sodas. On the other side of the room, a radio sat on a small table. Other than a few more pieces of furniture, the room was bare, the floor made of cement. We all gathered around. Kasarna's mother gestured for me to take a seat. I sat down on the sofa with both feet planted firmly on the floor, resting the bag beside me. My interpreter sat across from me. I reached in the bag, pulling out the gifts one by one: a stuffed leopard animal, a black doll with pretty, curly hair, two skirt sets, books and pencils. I watched Kasarna's face light up, a smile from ear to ear. For her mother, I brought cookies, candy and sugar. She was very appreciative, smiling as I handed her gifts. Kasarna came towards me, her tiny arms outstretched to embrace me, and I was overjoyed. Her mother picked up one of the outfits and led Kasarna into another room. When she emerged, she was wearing the outfit, only slightly oversized; not bad for a guess. Later, we went outside to take pictures. Kasarna sat atop a wooden table, resting in my arms. We gathered the two goats and put them in the picture too. The photos turned out beautiful. When the visit came to a close I expressed my appreciation for the time well spent. Shortly, we were on our way for the long journey back to town. My heart was warmed and moved in the joy of finally meeting the child I was so intrigued with. Mission accomplished as I headed to my hotel. I carried a bag full of snacks which were leftover from the visit. I offered some to the hotel doorman as I entered the lobby. He gladly took them. During the rest of my stay in Yogyakarta, I toured the shopping areas, purchasing a beautiful quilt by haggling for a fair price.

One evening I decided to have dinner in the Ambarrukmo Palace Hotel's restaurant. I gazed at the menu for several minutes while a waitress stood beside me. I didn't know what most of the items were. The only thing I recognized were the soft shell crabs. I decided to order those. I handed the menu to the waitress and she exited towards the kitchen. The meal was okay but soft shell crabs weren't one of my favorite seafood items.

The next evening I had planned to try dinner somewhere else but being unfamiliar with restaurant ratings I decided that the best idea would be to stay at my hotel. I returned to the restaurant for the second time. This time a young Indonesian man stood next to me, waiting for my selection. I once again looked over the menu, hoping to find something that I may have missed the night before. I ended up ordering the soft shell crabs again.

"Interesting, that is what you ordered last night," he said.

When the waiter walked away, I thought to myself. How did he know that? He didn't wait on me last night, a woman did. I came to the conclusion I was receiving more attention than I ever realized, right down to the meals I ordered. I guess I stuck out like a sore thumb.

Next I was headed for Bali, my final stop on my tour. Bali was a beautiful island. The natives made me feel very welcome. I was talking with one of the locals and he asked if I had a cigarette. I gave it to him and I also lit one for myself. In the distance I saw two Muslim women staring at me for a long time.

"Why are the women watching me so intently?" I asked.

"Women in this country don't smoke."

"I feel so embarrassed" I replied.

"Oh no, don't worry about it." "You can smoke."

"I don't want to make a spectacle of myself."

Eventually, the women turned their attention away from me. From then on I smoked my cigarettes out of the public eye.

The next evening I entered a restaurant to have dinner. There was a band playing on stage. After dinner I sat there listening to the music. They were playing popular American music. I was surprised to hear songs from back home. One of the musicians left the stage and came over to my table.

"Come on stage and sing with us," he invited.

"Oh no, I can't sing," I replied.

The young man wouldn't take no for an answer.

"What song do you know?"

I shrugged my shoulders. "I don't know what to sing."

After several attempts to think of something, I ended up with "Born Free."

I sang along with the band, trying to remember the words. At the conclusion of the song, I looked out into the audience. The few people who were there, were now gone.

"Oh my," I exclaimed. "I guess I ran them away."

The band members laughed and continued to play.

I rushed off the stage and returned to my table. A few minutes later, I was out the door.

When I returned to my room, I called my travel agent to check if he had found a way home for me. The phone rang and rang. I wonder why he isn't answering my calls. The next afternoon, I tried again. After several rings, I hung up. I started to worry about how I was going to get home. Lying in my bed, my mind started to think of my next move. Then I realized why the agent wasn't answering my calls. I had forgotten that this country was twelve hours ahead. It was four o'clock in the morning in the United States. I waited until 2:00 a.m. Indonesian time and called my agent. Finally, he answered.

"I called you a couple of times, forgetting about the twelve hour difference. Have you found a way for me to get home yet?" I inquired.

"I am working on it and I will call you back soon," he replied.

"Okay, I will stay close by the phone."

I needed to be out of here in the next two days. Anxiously I waited for the return call from my agent. When it came, he told me that the airlines had a flight for me and that I was to fly to Singapore.

"When you get to Singapore, go to the reservations desk. Instructions will be waiting for you there."

I thanked him for his help.

Two days later I arrived in Singapore. I approached the Reservations Desk and explained the particulars of my return home trip.

"Oh yes, Mrs. Bryant. We have a way home for you on business class. The ticket will cost $1300.00."

"No, absolutely not, I didn't pay that much for my round trip ticket to get here. I refuse to pay that kind of money to get home," I retorted.

"Well you can come back to the desk tomorrow morning and check to see if we have anything. Meanwhile, our airport offers Day Rooms for rent."

My body was starting to hurt. I needed to get somewhere and rest. I became frustrated. The hotel rooms I stayed in were colder than I desired. I tried to adjust the temperature but it had two settings, high and off. I was beginning to wonder if I were coming down with a cold. Thinking back several years, the last time cold air constantly blew down on me, my sickness turned into a major event. Fear started to grip me once more. I hope I don't ever go through an illness like that again.

I took the ticket agent's advice and went in search of a Day Room. When I found it, the woman in charge gave me instructions on how the rental worked and the hours I were allowed to stay including the checkout time.

I set my luggage down and relaxed on the bed. The room was beautifully decorated. Big soft fluffy pillows adorned the bed and I was soon fast asleep. The next morning, I remained in a lot of pain. I could barely walk and I was desperate to get home as quickly as possible. I was afraid I might be coming down with the flu. I returned to the Reservations Desk. Luckily, I was able to get a flight to Los Angeles.

When I presented my ticket, the agent told me I couldn't use it because it was destined for San Francisco.

"Why? The cost to fly to Los Angeles is the same price as here to San Francisco." I don't understand."

Another ticket agent was standing nearby listening.

"Miss, let me see your ticket please," he requested.

I handed the ticket to him.

"Miss, you are fine. You can use this ticket to fly to Los Angeles. I will rewrite this ticket."

The agent crossed off San Francisco and put in Los Angeles. He stamped it and I was good to go.

"Thank you for your knowledgeable help, sir."

I was never so glad to get on a flight. The pain in my body was getting severe. Thank God. I was finally on my way home. My cash was running out and when I arrived in Philadelphia, I had twenty dollars left in my purse. From Philadelphia to Indonesia and back, I had circled the globe. How interesting that was.

Back at the house, I climbed into bed to get some much needed rest. I reached for my cough medicine, covered my chest with vapor rub and crawled under the sheets. I stayed in bed for the next two days. I ate hot soup and drank plenty of tea. Luckily for me, my cold symptoms eased but the body pain remained.

When I was feeling better, I told my family and friends all about Indonesia. I distributed my souvenirs I had bought everyone. I had wood carvings, t-shirts, key chains and change purses that reminded me of my fascinating trip. I gave away everything except the beautiful quilt.

CHAPTER 11

In the months that followed, I concentrated my thoughts on what I felt may be God's purpose for my life. I followed my instincts in every decision I made. I spent time in silent prayer frequently and I listened for that still, small voice to speak to me. I sought direction in the midst of confusion. Often I felt alone and God was my only friend. At other times, an idle mind threatened me. I would have bouts of crying spells and I would find myself praying intensely. Through it all, I believed that I was slowly regaining my ability to see myself as the person I really was.

In the spring of 1989, nine years after being hired by the Postal Service, I enrolled in the Community College of Philadelphia. I always had the desire to go to college but it wasn't affordable to me when I graduated high school. Now I was able to pay my tuition and find out if I was really college material. I did well my first six semesters, acquiring a 4.0 average. I made the Dean's List in 1991-1992, excelling in English and foreign language. My English Literature instructor was very impressed with my writing technique. She encouraged me so much that I exceeded my own expectations.

One day, I tried my hand at writing poetry. With pen and paper in hand, I sat down to let my creativity flow. What transpired was a poem expressing my innermost feelings. When I had finished, I read back what I had written:

Inner Peace

I roam around in different places,
Searching for my spot;
A place where I can be myself,
To sit and dream a lot.

I rest beneath a sprawling tree,
In the valley far below;
And watch the birds fly overhead,
Not knowing where they go.

The moon and stars come out at night,
Against a blackened sky;
It penetrates my inner thoughts,
And I often wonder why.

All my hopes and dreams,
Are built on nothing less;
Then to find true inner peace,
Much love and happiness.

I decided to have my poem published in the National Library of Poetry. I am not what you would call a poet. This was my first poem and probably my last. What I discovered, was my ability to open my mind to endless possibilities.

My work hours conflicted with my study schedule. I had so much homework to turn in for each class that it soon became very difficult for me to go to work, study and get the proper amount of sleep. I decided to cut back on my classes and began taking just one class a semester. I was determined to keep going when some of my friends thought I would quit.

The only thing in my life I wanted to quit were those cancer sticks I constantly puffed on. One day I made up my mind to go "cold turkey" and that was it. For several days I fought withdrawal symptoms. It wasn't easy. My body went through changes, mood swings and the like. Every time I saw someone else smoke, the urge to pick up a cigarette was there. I could smell the aroma of a burning cigarette trying to lure me back in. I had to distance myself from places that reeked of smoke. It was an uphill battle. Eventually, I made it. I stopped smoking. A year passed without a cigarette. I thought I had the problem licked.

One night I was invited out to dinner with some of my friends. We went to a restaurant which served tasty burgers. We were ushered to a table and sat down. At each place setting, there were a pack of cigarettes. The restaurant was giving them away for free. I sat down and picked up the menu. I gave my order to the waitress. As I waited for my food to come, I toyed with the pack of cigarettes in my hand. Finally, I decided to open it. I was curious as to the taste. I never heard of the brand name before. I asked the waitress why they were giving away free cigarettes. She said it was a promotional offer. Finally I opened the pack and lit the cigarette. I took one puff, then two. I started to cough when I tried to inhale. I tried again. With each puff, it became easier. When we left the restaurant, I tossed the pack in my purse. The taste wasn't too bad. I smoked a few more then I headed to the store to buy the brand I was familiar with.

I was hooked, once again, on cigarettes. I had a new reason to renew my old habit; I was worried about Dian.

Dian was gone. The letters and phone calls ceased. I hadn't heard from him in four years. For a long time, I wondered how he was doing. Eventually, I stopped searching for Dian. I had to move on with my life.

I concentrated my efforts back on my college studies. I was thrilled about my educational pursuit. One afternoon I pulled into the parking garage but it was full. I had to exit and find a spot on the street. There was one spot left about ten feet from the garage exit. I parked my car and hurried to my class. When I returned to my car I unlocked the door and got in. I felt air blowing on me. I looked to my right. In the passenger seat laid my shattered car window on the passenger side. Glass was everywhere.

"Oh my God, I can't believe someone broke into my car!" I screamed.

Behind the passenger seat, there was a huge box containing a closet organizer I had purchased earlier in the day. I was surprised it wasn't stolen. I checked my glove compartment. All of my music tapes were gone and my radar detector. I sat there in disbelief. It took me several minutes to regain my composure. Then I exited the car and walked around to the passenger side. I gently tapped the remaining glass from the frame of the window and swept it from the seat. I thanked God that I was safe. From that day on I made sure I arrived at school early enough to get a parking space in the garage.

Whenever I couldn't cope with something, smoking helped alleviate the pain. My valuable items stolen from my car that day really annoyed me. I had an irreplaceable tape, "The Thanksgiving Song," amongst the missing items which stressed me tremendously. It seemed no matter the situation, I had a reason to smoke.

It was very easy for me to reach for a cigarette, especially when I was cramming for an exam. I realized that I was heavily addicted to cigarettes, once again, and I needed to find a way to limit the amount per day I was smoking. One of the goals I had set for myself was to quit altogether. I didn't like the fact that I was destroying my body. I smoked cigarettes since age fourteen and smoked a little marijuana too in my early twenties. I never became addicted to marijuana, so I quickly put it aside. Over the years, I developed a smokers' cough and a scratchy throat. My attempts to quit were futile at best. I thought I had it made when I stopped for a year, until that night out in the restaurant. With each passing day, I tried to break my addiction. I tried wearing the nicotine patches but I had an allergic reaction to them. My arms broke out with huge, red, raised circles. They itched very badly. Next, I tried the nicotine chewing gum, but it left a nasty, unbearable taste in my mouth. My next step was to go "cold turkey, again." That was a disaster, as well. I would tell myself, this is my last cigarette. When I got up in the morning I rushed to the ashtray and waste basket looking for cigarette butts. I would light the butt and puff on it, all the way to the filter. As soon as I stepped outside, I hurried to the nearest store to buy my next pack. I would say, I'll quit tomorrow or next week or on a specific date. Over and over I lied to myself. I prayed each time I lit a cigarette. God, I can do this, if only You would help me get through the withdrawal period.

One evening, I wasn't feeling well. It was May 16, 1993, four days after Janel's twenty-first birthday. My stomach was tight. I went into my bathroom and sat on the commode. I was constipated and turned on the spigot in the sink. For several seconds I let the water run. Nothing happened. I reached for my cigarettes. Only one remained in the pack. I lit the end of the cigarette and puffed on it several times. I smoked, cried and prayed for relief.

"God, please help me. I'm tired of smoking, Lord. I'm so tired. I want to regain my health. Please remove from me the urge to smoke."

The tears streamed down my face as I continued to puff on my last cigarette. Determined that this would really be my quitting point, I took it all the way to the filter. I inhaled deeply and slowly exhaled the smoke, savoring the final aroma of the tobacco. With my stomach in pain, I cried to the Lord once more. Please help me. In the next instance, my bowels broke loose.

"Thank you Lord, thank you."

When I returned to my bedroom, I climbed into bed and fell asleep. The next morning when I awoke, I swung my feet out of bed. I sat there for a few minutes before placing them on the floor. I didn't feel the urge to reach for a cigarette. I no longer searched the ashtray and trash can for cigarette butts. I went through my regular routine throughout the day. The cravings were gone, no withdrawal symptoms, whatsoever. God had answered my prayer. Had He not come, I would have been searching for a cigarette butt to light. He showed up, right on time.

A huge smile covered my face as I softly whispered, thank you Jesus for rescuing me. I never smoked another cigarette, ever. In the months that followed, I noticed the changes which were occurring within me. I could breathe better. My lungs were gradually being restored. The smokers' cough disappeared. My throat no longer felt scratchy. All these things were indicators that my health was improving. Once free of the addiction, I finally realized how bad cigarettes smelled to the non-smoker. It was in your hair, clothes, skin, carpet, hotel rooms, everywhere. It was so horrible, you could puke.

Three months later, I embarked on another cruise. I enjoyed the line Dian worked on. A new ship had joined the fleet. When my boyfriend and I arrived at the bottom of the gang plank, the passengers were slowly boarding. I looked up at the entranceway to the ship. I glimpsed a man standing there. His back was turned to me. He looked like Dian. No, it couldn't be. I thought my mind was playing tricks on me. I quickly dismissed the possibility. When I reached the top to step on board, I looked around at the staff. Dian was nowhere in sight. Miles looked at me, puzzled.

"What's wrong?" he asked.

"Nothing, just thought I saw Dian, but I guess I didn't," I replied. I erased it from my mind and continued to the cabin.

The next morning I prepared to go down to the dining room for breakfast. Miles had left the cabin earlier. When I opened the door to go out, he was coming up the corridor.

"What's wrong with you? If I didn't know better you look like you've seen a ghost."

"Dian is on this ship," he said.

"What are you talking about? You shouldn't have gone looking for him. You should have left well enough alone."

"If he is on the ship, you need to know, so I did some inquiring and he is really here."

"Fine, hopefully I won't run into him. Let's enjoy our cruise."

Easier said than done, Miles was befuddled by the whole thing. Later in the afternoon, I discovered him sitting in a chair on the lower level.

"Miles, what are you doing sitting there?" I asked.

"I'm waiting for Dian. One of the staff members went to find him. He should be here in a few minutes."

"You can sit here and wait if you want. I'm not." I turned to walk away.

"Gerri, turn around and look."

The staff member was talking with Dian. He pointed his hand in our direction. Dian spun around. A surprised look was evident on his face, as he walked toward us.

"Gerri, it's good to see you again."

Dian reached out to hug me and I kissed him on the cheek. Miles stood in the background watching us.

"It's good to see you again too, Dian. It's been a long time. I lost contact with you and I didn't know what to think. I'm glad you're okay."

"I know. I'm sorry. I went home and things changed."

"What happened?" I asked.

"I got married. I had to. My family was pushing me to do so."

"Well, I'm happy for you, Dian. Do you have any children yet?" I asked.

"Yes, two," he responded.

"That's nice. I would like to talk with you a little more. Can we meet out on deck this evening?"

"Yes, we can talk later."

He turned to Miles and shook his hand.

"Gerri is a nice, young lady. Please look after her. Enjoy your cruise."

Dian turned and walked away.

"Miles, I hope you're satisfied. Thanks for putting me on the spot like that."

"Well, don't get upset with me. You know you'd want to talk to him."

"From the very beginning I told you to drop the matter, but you chose to pursue it. I need to talk with Dian, so I hope you don't mind."

"Do what you feel is necessary."

From the look on his face he wasn't thrilled about it. He brought this on himself. He should have left well enough alone.

Around 10:00 p.m., I went to the upper deck to wait for Dian. I relaxed in a lounge chair. Two hours went by and Dian had not appeared. I soon fell asleep. When I awoke it was about 3:00 a.m. in the morning. If Dian came and found me asleep he may have thought it best not to awaken me. I don't know why he wouldn't try to arouse me. I decided to go back to my cabin. When I entered the room, Miles had his jaws tight.

"I thought you were going to spend the night on the deck. That must have been a hot conversation."

"Shut up, Miles. Dian never showed up. I fell asleep on deck."

"Now maybe you will forget about Dian. He's married now."

"You know what? I don't care. You started this ball rolling. Get over it. No one told you to look for Dian in the first place."

The next morning I ran into Dian.

"Where were you last night? I waited several hours for you and you didn't show up."

"I was there, Gerri. I found you sleeping and I didn't want to disturb you."

"Dian, you should have awakened me. That would've been okay."

"I'm sorry, Gerri. I thought it best to let you sleep."

I'm disappointed, Dian, but I understand."

"Gerri, please try to have a nice time. I hope I haven't caused any problems with you and your friend. He seems like a nice person."

"I'll handle him, Dian. It's okay. Hopefully, I'll see you around."

I turned to walk away. I could feel Dian's eyes on me as he watched me leave.

When I returned to my cabin, I could see that Miles was upset with me, even though he tried to hide it. He forced himself to hold conversations with me the rest of the trip. As far as I was concerned, the entire cruise was ruined. By the time we got off the ship we were barely speaking to each other. As we descended the stairway on our exit out, Dian was standing there as we passed. He extended his hand to Miles to shake his hand and Miles walked past Dian like he wasn't there. I embraced Dian one last time and wished him well.

"Take care of yourself, Dian."

"I will Gerri. I hope everything will be alright for you too, Gerri."

"Don't worry. It will. Thanks."

"Take care, Gerri."

That was the last I heard from Dian. He never called or wrote. I credit Miles with that because of his bad behavior towards Dian. I had to remind Miles of his circumstances. "You're married. I'm not. Don't forget it. I'm not attached at the hip to anybody."

Once back home, I had to decide what I wanted to do with the rest of my life. I was already bored with my dating situation. I was twelve years in and counting. Sooner or later I would make a decision. Until I figured out just what I really wanted, this was it for the time being. I had no intention of allowing Miles or anyone else control my life. Ultimately, I would make the final decision.

CHAPTER 12

It was June 1994. I flew into Narita Airport where I was met by Rev. Williams' friend who lived in Tokyo, He made me an itinerary to follow of the cities I desired to visit which included Tokyo, Kyoto and Hiroshima. I don't know what made me choose Japan, other than the fact I thought it was a nice country to visit. I planned on visiting many interesting places, such as gardens, temples and shopping malls.

Before leaving the United States, I purchased a rail pass to ride the different types of transportation for a discounted price. This rail pass was only offered to foreigners visiting Japan. This was the second trip I took without the benefit of family or friends accompanying me. I wasn't afraid to travel alone. I must admit. I had nerves of steel.

One day I decided to take a tour of one of many temples in the area where I was staying. The cab picked me up in the morning and dropped me off at the bottom of the temple. I spent about an hour touring the temples. When I returned to the street to take the cab back to my hotel, it was gone. I don't know what made me think he was going to sit there and wait for me. I tried to hail a cab, but each time the cabs were full of people and they passed me by. I didn't know how to call a cab using their public phones so I decided to start walking back towards my hotel. I had no idea where my hotel was from where I was so I searched the skyline to try and find the center of the city. The distance was further than I ever imagined. Each time I saw a cab coming, I put my hand up but there wasn't an empty cab anywhere. My only chance of getting back was to walk. It took me five hours, crossing over a one mile bridge in the process. I stayed focus, watching the skyline of the buildings to guide me safely back. It was 5:00 p.m. when I finally found my hotel. My feet hurt so much. The back of my ankles felt as if they were broken. When I reached my room, I headed for a long hot shower. Afterwards, I climbed into bed and was down for the count.

One day I took a ride on the subway system's loop train. I was on my way to Kyoto and was trying to familiarize myself with the train routes. Somehow I wound up on the loop train getting off where I had got on. I couldn't believe it when I made a complete loop and ended up where I started from. I got off and told personnel where I wanted to go and I was redirected on how to get there.

A lot of the restaurants were very pricey. I saw meals costing up to $100 per plate. I tried a sake drink while I was there. Sake was a Japanese fermented, alcoholic beverage made from rice. I couldn't acquire a taste for it, so I only had one sip. I found a McDonald's there so I tried the burger. It tasted like the ones in the U.S. I managed to afford a few Japanese meals.

Another interesting place I found myself in was a bed and breakfast house. It had four or five rooms available. The interesting thing was when you checked in you had to give the cook your breakfast order for the following morning. I didn't know that at the time so I couldn't eat breakfast there, I found another place to eat. What I did enjoy about the place was the level of respect for Japanese customs, such as, removing your shoes at the door and slipping your feet into available sandals that were provided for you. I found very few places in Japan where you could actually leave your shoes on.

My room had two windows. Out of one window I could hear a running brook splashing over rocks and out of the other could be heard the sound of a soft rain falling. The summer breeze blew through the open windows. I slept like a baby. It was the best peaceful sleep I have ever experienced in my entire life.

My next stop on my itinerary was Hiroshima. I boarded the Shinkansen or what is called the bullet train. That train ride was fantastic. It was very fast and quiet. I couldn't even hear the sound of the engine. It took five hours to get to Hiroshima. It was the best train ride imaginable.

Once in Hiroshima, I visited the museum there. The ravages of war were still evident in the remnants of burnt out buildings that remained. Hiroshima, on the other hand, had beautiful parks to tour. All in all, I found my visit to Japan fascinating.

I was happy to get home, safe and sound, once again. By this time I had completed my long distance travels to the other side of the world. I was now limiting myself only to cruise vacations and short flights.

In the summer of 1995, I boarded a plane destined for Aruba. I decided to take a much needed vacation. I wanted to go somewhere peaceful and serene. The warm, turquoise waters beckoned me, even though I couldn't swim. I would stick my feet in the water and watch the fish swim. Here I could relax and forget about everything back home except family and friends. The main purpose of my trip was to find a timeshare. I spent four days going to different presentations. I finally settled on the hotel where I was staying in the downtown area of Oranjestad. I was in the very heart of Aruba and centrally located to every amenity on the island. I wanted to come here to think and meditate without a lot of interruptions. I truly believed I could find some kind of peace within. I spent a lot of time walking along the path near the water. Huge iguanas perched on large boulders. Occasionally, I would toss small pieces of bread to them. Birds would gather around for crumbs of bread as well. It was fascinating to watch the interaction between the iguanas and the birds. The iguana would crawl across the walkway and stop in front of the bread. The birds plucked at every crumb they could find but they never went near the bread the iguana guarded. I thought that was so comical, just like people, territorial.

Satisfied with my timeshare purchase, I headed back to the United States. I felt relaxed knowing I had a hideaway spot nestled in the beautiful Caribbean that I could escape to.

In January 1996, I joined God's Community Choir. I would listen to this choir perform concerts all over the city of Philadelphia. My sister-in-law, Christine, was a member. I told her I was interested in joining. She was excited for me and told me to contact the directress. It was a great honor to become a part of this unique group. The members were like family to one another and we loved and respected each other so much. I love music and I love to sing. I've been involved with church choirs most of my life. I couldn't ask to be a part of a better group of people. The direction my life had taken was for the better. I don't believe they realized just how much they had been a huge part of my spiritual growth.

June 1997, I returned to Aruba for my first two-week vacation under my timeshare agreement. I decided I would come to Aruba every other year and run my weeks together to save on airfare and enjoy a longer stay. As soon as I had unpacked my bags, I hurried to the bus station. I needed groceries from the supermarket. The first thought was to save as much money as possible on meals. I selected about four or five restaurants to visit for dinner during my stay. Since I didn't mind cooking, most of my meals I prepared in my suite.

In the early evening I relaxed on my balcony overlooking the parking lot. I tried to purchase a suite on the ocean side but they were all sold out. I sipped on a glass of wine as the trade winds softly blew across the island. That breeze was so amazing. It's the first thing I noticed about the place on my very first visit when I rolled into port on a cruise ship. I was very careful in selecting the right hotel for me. I loved the fact that everything I needed was in walking distance except the supermarket. It was a very short ride by bus to get there. I was thrilled with the on-site amenities as well. I was blessed. I looked to my Savior every day for every important choice I made. I still had issues I was struggling with, but being here in Aruba, where I had nothing but time on my hands, helped me put things in perspective. Serenity is what I was looking for and it was what I found.

I called home almost every day to make sure everything was okay. I didn't like being away from my mother too long, but she always encouraged me to go and have a nice time.

She didn't want me worrying about her too much. My father wasn't in the best of health and I knew she had a lot to deal with concerning him.

Later in the week I walked down to the outdoor market. Souvenirs of every kind lined the streets. I bought several T-shirts and caps, key chains and other trinkets for my family and friends. Across the street from the market was what I called the sister hotel. It fell under the same ownership as my place and it housed an indoor shopping mall with lots of upscale shops. On the second level of the hotel was the entrance to the casino which I visited frequently. Also there was a huge theater for the entertainment shows.

On my hotel property was a huge fenced in area where Elsa lived. She was a beautiful tiger trained to perform in the entertainment shows on the island. Many tourists took photos alongside her. I asked the trainer if she was well fed before I stepped into the pen. I climbed up on the table and sat next to Elsa with my hand on the lower back of her head. The photo turned out beautiful. I took many pictures everywhere I went. When I returned home I had a camera loaded with memories of my wonderful vacation.

Aruba was important because it allowed me to free my mind of the day to day problems that faced me back home. I was in a place where I could feel free to let my hair down and just be me. Relaxing was something that didn't happen often, so every chance I got to escape the cruelties of life, I took it.

Most of my insecurities stemmed from the conditions of my relationships. I harbored a lot of resentment that I couldn't seem to shake, no matter how I tried. I prayed often to God about my feelings, yet something kept me from releasing the pain and totally committing my fears to Him. Sometimes I asked myself, does God still love me when I find it too hard to love my enemies?

December 29, 1998, my father passed. He never formed that bond with me that I needed growing up, probably due to his alcoholism. Although I had a deep respect for him, I never experienced the closeness that I shared with my mother. I loved him despite his shortcomings because he was my father. I recalled the time when he taught me how to ride my bike. When he thought I was ready for two wheels, he removed the training wheels from the back. He grasped the handle bars to steady me until I could balance the bike on my own, then he let go. How proud I was at my accomplishment. As I grew older, he tried to make up for lost time. When I was old enough, he taught me how to play checkers. In the beginning he would win all the time, until I learned the strategy of the game. After a while I started to win a lot. I often thought he allowed me to win on purpose. When I became grown, he would send me to the seafood stores to buy bushels of live crabs. I would bring them home and he would show me how to cook them. Once in a while, one would get away and scurry across the floor. He would chase it down until he caught it. We would laugh and have a good time. Even though those moments were few and in between, I remember them as special. It was during those times, that I really got to know him.

In June 1999, I went back to the island of Aruba, my favorite vacation spot. This time I wasn't able to get my two weeks at the same hotel. The first week I stayed at my place and the second week I went to another hotel. I took a cab from my hotel to the second location. This hotel had a non-denominational chapel on the grounds. When I was out exploring one day, I entered the chapel to pray. The place was empty. I looked around at the beautiful stained glass windows. It was small yet comfortable and it had several pews inside. I walked towards the front and slid into a pew on the second row and sat there for several minutes in silence. Then I knelt down to pray. I had specific things I was praying over, especially my situation with dating married men. I wanted to end my relationships with them and make a different commitment to my Lord and Savior, Jesus Christ. I asked God for guidance as I prayed for answers to all of my dilemmas. When I had finished, I rose to my feet and left the chapel. I felt refreshed with a new spirit. When I returned to the U.S., I knew in my heart, for the first time, I had real purpose for my life.

November 1999, I went to have a stress test done. I was forty-five years old. I don't know what prompted it, but my primary doctor felt it was necessary that I have one. I made the appointment with a cardiologist whom she recommended. That morning I headed into the health center to prepare for my test. The assistant hooked me up to the monitors and turned the machine on. I was a minute into the test when the speed was increased. I started walking faster when all of a sudden the cardiologist stopped the machine.

"Take her down," he instructed the assistant.

She unhooked the monitor and led me to a chair.

"How are you feeling?" the doctor asked.

"I'm good, just a little tired," I replied.

He continued to ask me questions about my experience on the treadmill. A few minutes later I saw a gurney arrive at the door.

"What's that for?" I asked.

"It's for you, Mrs. Bryant. I can't allow you to go home. You must be admitted into the hospital."

"Huh? Are you kidding?" I asked.

"No," he responded.

He showed me the EKG tape. The lines were all over the place. I was transferred from the chair to the gurney and the attendant rolled me to the Emergency Unit where they attached monitors and an IV to my hand. I was rolled into a room where I remained for several hours. I was alone for so long, I thought they had forgotten about me. I tried to get the attention of staff walking by but to no avail. It was close to five o'clock and I was getting hungry and angry. Finally, around 5:30 p.m., I was advised that I would be transported by ambulance to the hospital, a few blocks away. The ride seemed like it took forever. Once at the hospital, they didn't have a bed for me, so they left me in ICU until they could find one. Meanwhile I called my family and a couple of friends to let them know what had happened. I requested some Chinese food be brought to me. I didn't have anything to eat all day and I was very hungry. When my friends arrived, I took the bag and started to open it. The shrimp lo-main smelled so good. My room was stationed right across from the nurses' station. They must have smelled it too. One of the nurses got up and rushed into the room.

"No, no, no, Mrs. Bryant. You can't have that. I will find you something to eat," she said.

"Finally, I'm getting some attention around here," I said to my friends.

I closed the food container and handed it back to my friends. When they had left, the nurse walked in a few minutes later with a roast beef sandwich. I looked at it. It was dry, no mayo nor mustard on it. I made a face as I tried to down the dry sandwich that got stuck in my throat. It was the worst, as I washed it down with water.

"Ugh," I thought. "Hospital food is horrible, to say the least."

A couple days later, Miles walked into the room, carrying a card and small plant in his hand.

"How did you find out I was here?" I questioned.

"I called your job when I couldn't find you," he said.

Miles, we are not together anymore. I appreciate your concern but it wasn't necessary for you to come. But now that you're here, would you do me a favor, please?'

"And what's that?"

"Please take my check to the bank and deposit it for me. I need to pay my bills."

I handed the check and deposit slip to Miles."

"Thank you. I appreciate it."

I had ended the relationship with Miles. I prayed a lot. I prayed for change. I wanted a closer relationship with God and that meant making some lifestyle choices that would be pleasing to Him.

I spent the next few days taking all kinds of tests. I was tired of them poking me with needles, waking me up every two hours and a blood pressure cuff squeezing my arm every hour. It was crazy. One day, I decided to get out of bed and drag my IV drip stand into the restroom. When I emerged from the doorway a nurse came running into the room.

"Mrs. Bryant, what are you doing?"

"I went to the restroom."

"The doctor wants you to use a bed pan," she insisted.

"I'm fine. I don't need a bed pan. Where were all of you in 1973 when my heart felt like it would jump out of my chest? I questioned. That was the time I needed attention. I thought I was dying."

The nurse helped me back into bed.

"Mrs. Bryant, please call for assistance before getting up again," she warned with a stern look.

My cardiologist paid me a visit on day five. He had me take another stress test and walk up and down the corridor until he was satisfied with the results. He wrote a prescription for metoprolol and sent me home.

It was December 1999, a year since my father's passing. My father came to mind this morning as I prepared to go to work. Christmas was fast approaching. It was a dry, snowless winter thus far. I cracked my window to let in the cold, crisp air as I drove down Cheltenham Avenue. The streets were dark, except for the occasional street lamp that shone ever so often. It was 3:30 a.m. There weren't many cars on the road this time of morning. I turned the radio on to break the silence. Gospel music played softly as I adjusted the volume to a comfortable listening level.

On this particular morning, I had the stretch of road to myself. I was moving at a speed of 40 mph. In the distance I could see the headlights of another vehicle approaching. As the vehicle drew closer, I noticed it was a large, white van. It was just the two of us on the road. All of a sudden, the van left its lane and headed straight at me. I had two choices to make, either swerve left or right. Since there was nothing behind him, I chose to go left. I turned the wheel in that direction and ran up on a parking area. I slammed on my brakes to avoid running into the storefront wall. As I looked back in my rear view mirror, I watched the van go through the intersection in my lane. Once completely through, the vehicle recovered and got back on the correct side of the road. The near head-on collision seemed almost intentional. I didn't know whether the driver was ill, under the influence or had fallen asleep. I was blessed to be able to avoid what could have been a fatal accident.

"Thank you Lord for keeping me safe," I uttered aloud.

I sat there on the parking lot for several seconds, regaining my composure before continuing on. Once at work, I picked up my timecard and punched in, glad to be still amongst the living.

June 2001 found me back in Aruba. I had a two week stay at my own hotel this time. I was in deep meditation most of this trip. I remembered my last visit when I found the non-denominational chapel on the grounds of the other hotel I stayed at. I wanted to return there so I planned to stop at the hotel while I was up at that end of the island.

Upon arriving to the non-denominational chapel, I wrapped my fingers around the door knob and turned. With everything quiet inside and no one there, I pulled the door towards me. I was glad to have the place to myself, once again. I sat down in a pew at the front of the chapel. I pondered upon what I would say to God. Then I knelt down to pray.

Satisfied with my purpose for returning to the chapel one more time, I boarded a plane to head back to the United States. Each time I came to Aruba, the trip seemed too short. I wanted to stay here forever but that was a dream, not a reality. All in all, I accomplished my heart's desire.

One month later, July 10, 2001 was a very important date in my life. I stood in my bedroom, in front of the bed. I reached for my pillow and placed it on the floor. It would act as a cushion for my knees against the hardwood floor. I lowered myself on the pillow, making sure I was in a comfortable position. I rubbed the inside of my hands together several times as I prepared to fold them in a prayer position. Then I began to pray. This was a special prayer, one like no other. It was a serious prayer and one not to be entered into lightly, but fully aware of possible consequences. Ecclesiastes 5:4-5 says–"So when you make a promise to God, don't delay in following through, for God takes no pleasure in fools. Keep all the promises you make to him. It is better to say nothing than to promise something that you don't follow through on."

At the conclusion of my prayer, with tears of joy in my eyes, I stood up with my hands raised upward, thanking my Lord, thy God, for my life, health and an abundance of blessings. Most importantly, the prayer I prayed was a vow of celibacy.

I had broken off my relationship with Miles two years prior. Any other previous relationships were broken as well. I was now alone, living a life without any mate whatsoever.

I had reached the point in my life where I could make this commitment to God. I had thought about it long and hard. I was ready to live up to my commitment with no hesitation and no regrets.

It was early spring, 2003. I drove down Cheltenham Avenue. It was a route I traveled often to get to work, or to the mall. Once in a while my mind would wander to the sad places in my heart. Sometimes I would shed tears and I would take the back of my hand and wipe my eyes to clear my vision. I pushed my CD into the player. Soft instrumental hymns began to play. Music always calmed me down with its soothing effect. I was riding along and had just crossed a three way intersection at Cheltenham, Ogontz and Upsal when I decided I wanted to switch lanes. I checked my rear view mirrors for signs of other traffic. I didn't see anyone behind me. I turned my wheel to the right. Just as I was about to move into the right hand lane, a gust of wind came out of nowhere. I felt a force pushing against the car, preventing me from moving over as I continued to move forward. I turned my head to the right in time to see a car zipping by me at 35-40 mph.

"Oh my God," I cried.

That car was in my blind spot and I never saw it coming. Once again, I was under the protection of the Almighty from an unseen danger.

"Thank you, Lord," I cried as I continued to my destination. Through all my troubles and disappointments I had experienced thus far, God still had my back.

In June 2003 I stood on the balcony of my hotel room in Aruba, looking out over the complex. This year I came here with uncertainty because I was very concerned about my mother. I believed she was okay because Janel and her family were now living in the house with her. My mother wasn't alone and that was important, yet I still worried.

I called Janel on the phone.

"Did mom eat her dinner?"

"Yes, she had fish. She likes that a lot," Janel replied.

"Please make sure she takes her medicine,"

"I will, mom," Janel promised.

I hung up, assured that my mother was okay. I called home every night and asked the same question until I could return home and see for myself.

My mother was ninety years old. Her health was starting to slowly decline. The family kept a watchful eye over her and we made sure her needs were met. She loved to look out the window and sat in the chair most of the day, radio playing. I was very protective of her. She was my mother whom I loved and respected very much. As a child, she tended to my every need and now I was willing to do the same for her.

The following year, my mother suffered many mini strokes and would pass out for several minutes at a time. The ambulance was summoned to the house on a few occasions to take her to the hospital. She would be there two or three days, sometimes before sending her back home. I stayed by my mother's side as much as I could. Janel living with her gave me some comfort in knowing she had someone around most of the time.

Christmas 2004, the family carried gifts to mom. She now resided in a nursing home. I visited my mother three to four days a week. Janel, I and other family members divided our time as much as possible. We gathered around her bedside and watched her open her gifts. A lot of her strength was gone as we watched her slowly struggle with the gift wrap. She was happy to see her family around her, especially her great-grandchildren.

Early March, 2005, the nursing home informed me that my mother's condition was deteriorating rapidly and they were suggesting hospice care for her. Something in my head told me to check into her life insurance policies to make sure she had adequate coverage. When I called the companies, they told me that she had outlived her policies and no longer had coverage. I couldn't believe the response I received. I never heard of such a thing.

Then I began to pray. I prayed to God that he would keep my mother alive until I could get the money for burial expenses. The following day, I applied for a loan from my thrift savings account to cover the cost. It took about eight days for me to receive it. In the meantime, I prayed over and over again for God to keep her on this side of the living. When the check arrived, I deposited in my bank account. I was well prepared for her pending death, and I was so thankful to my Lord and Savior for sparing me any more grief than I could bear. My mother told me before she died, she wanted a nice funeral. I told her, it would be nothing short of beautiful.

On March 18th, hospice care alerted me that my mother was in a comatose state and hard to arouse her. I knew the end was near. The next evening, I went to the nursing home around seven in the evening. I heard that people in a comatose state can hear even though they may not be able to respond. If that was the case, I sat next to my mother and talked to her. I told her about her great-grandchildren, that she didn't have to worry about them. They would be okay. I prayed over my mother and sang hymns to her. I tried to climb in the bed next to her but there just wasn't enough room for the two of us, so I held her hand instead. It was 10:00 p.m. I was getting tired. My body started to hurt and I was getting uncomfortable in the chair I was seated in. I kissed my mother on the cheek.

"I will see you in the morning, mom. I love you."

I left the room knowing that God had my mother cradled in his arms. At 3:00 a.m. Mar. 20th, I was awakened by a ringing telephone. I didn't have to look over to see who was calling me. I knew. I picked up the phone. I was at peace at the delivery of the news. I knew my mother had no more worries. She was definitely at peace with God.

I did everything I could for my mother while she was living. We had that special mother and daughter bond. I had no regrets. My mother's service was the Saturday between Good Friday and Easter. What a perfect time to be in the midst of the Passion Season commemoration of our Lord and Savior, Jesus Christ.

July 2007, I was appointed to the position of church secretary. Due to illness, the former secretary could no longer fulfill her duties. At first I was hesitant because I lacked the secretarial skills and confidence needed to take on such a huge responsibility, but my pastor had the vision to believe that I could succeed. Then and only then, did I feel this was God's purpose for me.

Early August of 2008, I conferred with my gynecologist about fibroid tumors which were bothering me for a while. I wanted to know her honest opinion about what route to go in treatment for this condition. She laid out all of my options.

"What would you do, if you had to make this decision?" I asked her.

"I would let the fibroids shrink over a period of time," she responded.

"I have tried that for the past three years and some of the tumors are still the same size. I have been losing blood a lot. I'm starting to become anemic."

"You can take iron pills for the anemia," she said.

"Well, I am at the age now where my child bearing days are over. I will give it some more thought before I make my final decision."

I left her office with the literature she had given me. I read it and weighed my options carefully. I still couldn't make up my mind.

One day I was at work when I started losing blood heavily. It continued every day for a month. I called my doctor to inform her that I was coming up on the 31st day. She immediately scheduled me for surgery.

November 11, 2008, I entered the hospital for a hysterectomy. I was prepped for surgery and rolled into the operating room shortly after 10:00 a.m. When I awoke it was 7:00 p.m. I felt my bed being rolled down a hallway and into a private room as I started to arouse. I was so sleepy from the anesthesia. I opened my eyes long enough to see the nurse pushing the bed. She introduced herself to me and made sure I was comfortable before leaving. I returned to my slumber state.

My doctor came to visit me the next morning. She explained to me that she found a tumor the size of an orange covering my left ovary. A biopsy was done and it turned out that it was benign. I recalled, over the years during ultrasound tests, how the technicians would ask me if I had my ovary removed. I would say no. This explains why they couldn't see my ovary. If it had not been for the surgery, this tumor may not have been found. God's blessing was upon me once again as I yielded to my intuitiveness.

December 12, 2013, an ordinary day, I was working in my house. A cleaning crew assisted me in the preparation of putting things in order. A lot of foot traffic in and out the door, as heavy furniture was carried from room to room.

My hair fell down on my neck. I pushed it back up. In doing so, my hand brushed against the back of my shoulder. My skin felt strange. There was a cluster of bumps nestled between the nape of my neck and my shoulder blade. When I arrived home later that evening, I picked up a mirror to see what the bumps revealed. I was concerned. I thought I knew what it was but I needed confirmation.

At 12:40 p.m. the next day I called my doctor's office. I told the receptionist I needed an appointment as soon as possible.

"Are you having any symptoms, Ms. Bryant?" she asked.

"Yes, I have a rash that needs to be diagnosed," I answered.

"The soonest I can get you in would be December 16th," she said. "Let me check to see if there are any cancellations. Please hold the line," she requested.

"Okay," I replied.

I was put on hold for about two minutes. When the receptionist came back on the line she asked if I could get there by 1:00 p.m.

"Yes, I can. Thank you," I replied.

"The doctor had a cancellation that occurred at 12:30 p.m. She will slide you into that slot."

"Thanks again. I'm on my way," I said.

My doctor's office was down the street from my house. At one o'clock, I walked through the reception area of the office and signed in at the desk. No one else occupied the waiting area.

A few minutes later I was ushered into the examination room. When the doctor came in, she took one glance at my neck.

"Ms. Bryant, you have shingles," she said.

"I thought that might be the case, but I wasn't sure," I told her.

"When did you notice the rash?"

"I discovered it yesterday, accidently while pushing up strands of hair that fell on my neck."

"Well hopefully, we caught this in time. We can treat this with medication within the first forty-eight hours to prevent the illness from spreading further. I'm going to call the pharmacist and put this prescription in right away. Take one tablet every twelve hours for seven days," the doctor instructed.

Two hours later, I picked up the medication from the drugstore. At 4:00 p.m. I swallowed my first dose. I adhered to the instructions explicitly. I had no further signs of the illness. It was like it never occurred. The rash remained visible for about ten days.

I thanked God for the nudge. Most people don't notice the early signs until it's too late. Being that this illness is a virus, it can attack anywhere in the body and could have permanent complications.

In this book, I revealed the amazing experiences that ultimately happened to me. If it weren't for those revelations which inspired this book, it may never have been written.

As a follower of Christ, it is my responsibility to share my Christian faith with anyone who is open to it; however, it is up to each individual to choose the path which they believe to be relevant in respect to their own spiritual journey.

I can certainly attest to the goodness of God in His infinite love, wisdom and power throughout my life, for which I am so very grateful… and the journey continues.

EPILOGUE

It is my pleasure to have known and worked with Ms. Bryant during the course of my ministerial activities—pastoral, educational and social—for almost three decades. I know her as a person of genuine faith, one who is willing to help in advisory roles to parents, adolescents and adults (including seniors like myself). In light of her humility and dedication, she is a miracle herself. I would have not been able to carry out the ministries in my own life had it not been for her strong assistance for my family. I hope to see another book by her on miraculous deeds of God through her as she shifts her focus through evangelism.

www.ingramcontent.com/pod-product-compliance
Lightning Source LLC
LaVergne TN
LVHW011940070526
838202LV00054B/4729